Illustrated

STORIES *from the*
BOOK *of* MORMON

Illustrated STORIES *from the* BOOK *of* MORMON

Volume 8

Dr. Clinton F. Larson, *Narrative and Editing*
Professor of English, Brigham Young University

Joseph N. Revill, *Correlator and Writer; Associate Editor*

Stuart Heimdal, *Artist and Art Director*

Dr. Paul Cheesman, *Director of Research*

Published by
PROMISED LAND PUBLICATIONS, INC.
Salt Lake City, Utah

FIRST EDITION VOLUME 8 1970

Lithographed in U.S.A.
PROMISED LAND PRESS
Salt Lake City, Utah

Contents

Foreword

" . . . can ye imagine yourselves brought before the tribunal of God with your souls filled with guilt and remorse, having a remembrance of all your guilt, yea, a perfect remembrance of all your wickedness, yea, a remembrance that ye have set at defiance the commandments of God?"

Alma 5:18

As we approach the task of illustrating the activities of Alma in the Book of Mormon, we find it extremely difficult to portray wholly the message he so forcefully gives to his people.

Perhaps there has never been a better sermon on repentance and the universal need for it than is contained in the fifth chapter of Alma, covered in this volume. Do not miss reading this forceful chapter.

It is difficult and often impossible to illustrate some doctrinal subjects. It becomes necessary, therefore, that one acquaint himself with these points through the written word.

When we view our world conditions and see so many of God's children departing into forbidden paths, we realize that Alma was speaking and writing to us and our day as well as to his own people. We will all journey from this life on the same pathway; we will all be called on for an accounting before the tribunal of God. If we can resolve from this day forward to observe the commandments as given us from God, and thus by repentance merit his merciful consideration, what happiness and joy will be ours hereafter!

— The Publishers

Acknowledgments

Again we are pleased to acknowledge the contribution that has been made by our advisory board in interpreting and researching the material contained in Volume 8 of *Illustrated Stories from the Book of Mormon*.

To Dr. Paul R. Cheesman, our director of research, Dr. Sidney B. Sperry, Dr. Ellis T. Rasmussen, Dr. Ross T. Christensen, Golden Berrett, and Joseph N. Revill of our advisory board, we express our heartfelt thanks for the many hours of labor that have gone into this beautiful volume.

To Dr. Clinton F. Larson we are again indebted for his masterful handling of the narrative accompanying the illustrations contained in this volume. We sincerely appreciate the contribution Dr. Larson is making to Mormon Literature.

The illustrations for this volume are the works of Stuart Heimdal, Vernon Murdock, and Keith Christensen. To each of these men we express our deep appreciation for their outstanding and beautiful contributions.

The historical sketch, "Portraits in Words," and the correlating material for this volume, are from the pen of Joseph N. Revill. "Pearls for Thought" in this volume were researched and prepared by Dr. Paul R. Cheesman. To each we express our appreciation.

—*The Publishers*

A Short History of The Church of Jesus Christ of Latter-day Saints

CHAPTER 8

By Joseph N. Revill

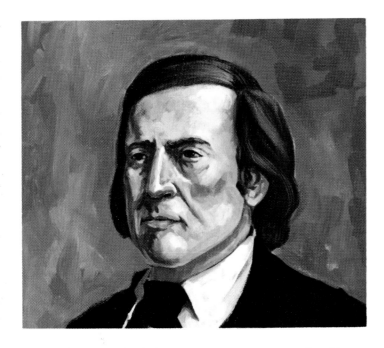

The arrival of the pioneer company in the Great Salt Lake Valley on July 22, 23, and 24, 1847, was the beginning of one of the great colonization periods in America's history. The season was late for planting, but the Saints needed to preserve and increase their seed supply. One of the first acts in the unfolding drama was the beginning of planned irrigation in modern times on the western hemisphere. Dams were thrown across the streams and the water flooded over the hard, parched ground, thus making it possible to plow without breaking the implements.

July 25 was the Sabbath, and no work was done that day. Within the circle of pioneer wagons, the Saints rejoiced, and in worship gave thanks for their blessings and the open spaces of the wilderness west now available to them for their refuge.

President Young, having seen the vision of the Saints' future, was convinced that the site selected for the city was the best. Exploring parties in various directions into the valley and canyons proved him correct, and a plan was adopted for the orderly planning and building of the city with proper utilization of the lands and water.

Along with building homes, farms, and businesses for themselves, one project was of utmost importance to the Saints. That subject was the building of a Temple to the Lord. On the 28th of July, President Young and those Apostles in the valley, walked northward from the encampment and between two forks of City Creek, President Young stuck his cane into the earth and said, "Here we will build the Temple, the city will be laid out from this center east, west, north, and south." In spite of the hardships and suffering of these people, they were still concerned for their spiritual future and would speedily go about building the Temple. But they faced an approaching winter, their supplies scanty, and the need for protection against the inclement weather and the possible troubles from the Indian tribes that were numerous in the region also had to be considered.

On August 1, a special meeting was held and a decision was made to construct a log and adobe fortress that could provide both shelter and refuge from Indian trouble. By August 10, work was underway on this structure.

President Young was concerned for the welfare of the hundreds of other pioneers that were following and would soon arrive in the Valley.

August 2 found Ezra T. Benson, with a company of horsemen, heading back toward Winter Quarters with instructions to obtain the names and numbers of the Saints in the various camps, as well as to their general condition, and the number of wagons, oxen, horses, and cattle making this trek. If there were any in need of help, they were to receive it, if at all possible.

On August 16 and 17, seventy-one men, thirty-three wagons, fourteen mules, and ninety-two yoke of oxen left the valley on the journey to help these other companies reach safety. On the 26th, President Young and the Apostles started back to Winter Quarters to organize and direct the thousands of immigrants yet waiting the time for their move westward. This journey turned out to be very eventful. As they traveled eastward, they met numerous wagon trains wending their way toward the great valley of refuge. In all, they passed more than fifteen hundred men, women, and children, five hundred-sixty wagons, and more than five thousand head of livestock.

The last part of the journey was on foot for many of the brethren. The group had lost some of their horses to thieving Indians and others to the harshness of the journey. This group arrived in Winter Quarters on October 31, with great rejoicing.

The year 1847 came to a close with 2,095 pioneers living within the improvised quarters in Salt Lake Valley.

After the martyrdom of the Prophet Joseph and Hyrum Smith in 1844, the Council of the Twelve Apostles had been sustained by the membership as the presiding council of the Church. On December 5, 1847, at Kanesville, Iowa, Brother Brigham Young was selected by the members of the Quorum to be the President of the Church. He chose as Counsellors, Heber C. Kimball and Willard Richards. This action was unanimously sustained by the membership in a conference held on the Iowa side of the Missouri River as well as subsequently at Garden Grove, Iowa, and in the Salt Lake Valley.

The time spent by the Saints at Winter Quarters had proven beneficial. An abundant crop had been gathered and the majority of the thousands gathered there were rapidly preparing for their westward move to the Great Basin.

In June, 1848, Brother Brigham Young and Heber C. Kimball left Winter Quarters at the head of two

great companies of pioneers numbering more than two thousand souls, with over six hundred wagons and literally thousands of heads of livestock and numerous fowl.

In July, President Willard Richards left Winter Quarters at the head of a company of five hundred souls and one hundred sixty-nine wagons.

Meanwhile, the Saints at Salt Lake were experiencing a great test of faith. The late arrival of pioneers in 1847 had resulted in a very poor harvest of crops. The growing season of 1848 was vitally important to them and to the many thousands who were soon to join them in the valley. Crops in May and June looked good. There were five thousand one hundred thirty-three acres planted, and an abundant harvest looked assured. Their feelings of security were short lived, however, when great hordes of crickets began to move down the mountain sides into the fields, devouring everything before them.

The Saints marshalled themselves and fought day and night to stem the tide of the voracious pests. They dug ditches and filled them with water, but to no avail; they beat them with brooms, shovels, and clubs, but it was no use. The pests just kept coming — more and more of them. In despair the Saints had only one thing they could do. They turned to the Lord, who had led them to this valley of refuge. Their prayers were heard. The sky became dark with thousands of seagulls that began to soar over the fields. Some Saints wondered if the birds were coming to eat what little the crickets were leaving! They then saw the seagulls devouring the crickets by the thousands! The birds gorged themselves on the pests, flew off to some water and vomited, again returned to devour more crickets. This miracle of the seagulls continued day after day until all the crickets were destroyed and some of the vital crops saved.

What a testimony that these were God's people, that He had led them here, that He would preserve them and aid them, and they would build up Zion in the midst of the mountains.

In September, Presidents Young and Kimball arrived with their respective companies. They had experienced hardship, they had brought many poor with them, and their trail was frequently marked with graves. But the spirits of these pioneers were kept high by the inspiration of their great leaders.

Frequently they could be heard singing William Clayton's inspiring song:

Come, come, ye Saints, no toil nor labor fear;
But with joy wend your way.
Though hard to you this journey may appear,
Grace shall be as your day.

'Tis better far for us to strive
Our useless cares from us to drive;
Do this, and joy your hearts will swell —
All is well! all is well!

Why should we mourn or think our lot is hard?
'Tis not so; all is right.
Why should we think to earn a great reward,
If we now shun the fight?
Gird up your loins; fresh courage take;
Our God will never us forsake;
And soon we'll have this tale to tell —
All is well! all is well!

We'll find the place which God for us prepared,
Far away in the West,
Where none shall come to hurt or make afraid;
There the Saints will be blessed.
We'll make the air with music ring,
Shout praises to our God and King;
Above the rest these words we'll tell —
All is well! all is well!

And should we die before our journey's through,
Happy day! all is well!
We then are free from toil and sorrow, too;
With the just we shall dwell!
But if our lives are spared again
To see the Saints their rest obtain,
O how we'll make this chorus swell —
All is well! all is well!

Several months after Presidents Young, Kimball, and Richards had left Winter Quarters with their large companies of Saints, an event occurred at Winter Quarters which cheered the hearts of all the members of the Church throughout the world. The former second Elder in the Church, Oliver Cowdery, a witness to the Book of Mormon, a joint receiver of the Aaronic and Melchizedek Priesthoods at the hands of heavenly messengers, and one who wrote nearly every word of the Book of Mormon as it fell from the lips of the Prophet Joseph Smith as he translated it from the plates, returned and asked to be received back into membership in the Church. (See "Portraits in Words.")

Having been separated from the Church for nearly ten years and like the prodigal son of the Savior's parable (Luke 15), Oliver Cowdery had now seen the error and folly of his ways, and in humility he wanted to start over in the kingdom of God. To his eternal credit we can say that though he was outside the Church and had many opportunities to do so Oliver Cowdery never denied his testimony of the truth of the events of Church history of which he was a part, including the coming forth of the Book of Mormon.

Another interesting event had occurred in California involving members of the Mormon Battalion, who, having completed their enlistment period in the Army, were advised by President Young, who sent Captain James Brown to California from Salt Lake with instructions for them to seek work in California through the winter of 1847-48 and then journey to the Salt Lake Valley. While thus employed, some of these men near Sacramento were responsible for the discovery of gold, which precipitated the gold rush of

1849. This event was of importance to the Saints and did aid them in their subsequent struggle to establish themselves in their mountain retreat. From James Brown's autobiography we find an excellent description of the conditions of this period of time.

"The winter of 1848-49 was quite cold. Many people had their feet badly frozen. For one, the writer suffered so severely from this cause that he lost every nail from the toes of both feet. In February and March there began to be some uneasiness over the prospects, and as the days grew warmer the gold fever attacked many so that they prepared to go to California. Some said they would go only to have a place for the rest of us; for they thought Brigham Young too smart a man to try to establish a civilized colony in such a 'God-forsaken country,' as they called the valley. They further said that California was the natural country for the Saints; some had brought choice fruit pips and seed, but said they would not waste them by planting in a country like the Great Salt Lake Valley; others stated that they would not build a house in the valley, but would remain in their wagons, and in the spring would be

going on to California, Oregon or Vancouver's Island; still others said they would wait awhile before planting choice fruits, as it would not be long before they would return to Jackson County, Missouri . . .

"It was at this time of gloom that President Young stood before the whole people, and said, in substance, that some people had misgivings, and some were murmuring, and had not faith to go to work and make their families comfortable; they had got the gold fever and were going to California. Said he: 'Some have asked me about going. I have told them that God has appointed this place for the gathering of his Saints, and you will do better right here than you will by going to the gold mines. Some have thought they would go there and get fitted out and come back, but I told them to stop here and get fitted out. Those who stop here and are faithful to God and his people will make more money and get richer than you that run after the god of this world; and I promise you in the name of the Lord that many of you that go thinking you will get rich and come back, will wish you had never gone away from here, and will long to come back, but will not be able to do so. Some of you will come back, but your friends who remain here will have to help you; and the rest of you who are spared to return will not make as much money as your brethren do who stay here and help build up the Church and Kingdom of God; they will prosper and be able to buy you twice over. Here is the place God has appointed for his people.

"'We have been kicked out of the frying pan into the fire, out of the fire into the middle of the floor, and here we are and here we will stay. God has shown me that this is the spot to locate his people, and here is where they will prosper; he will temper the elements for the good of his Saints; he will rebuke the frost and the sterility of the soil, and the land shall become fruitful. Brethren, go to, now, and plant out your fruit seeds.'

"Stretching his arms to the east and to the west, with his hands spread out, he said:

"'For in these elements are not only all the cereals common to this latitude, but the apple, peach and plum; yea, and the more delicate fruits, the strawberry and raspberry; and we will raise the grapes here and manufacture wine; and as the Saints gather here and get strong enough to possess the land, God will temper the climate, and we shall build a city and a temple to the Most High God in this place. We will extend our settlements to the east and west, to the north and to the south, and we will build towns and cities by the hundreds, and thousands of the Saints will gather in from the nations of the earth. This will become the great highway of the nations. Kings and emperors and the noble and wise of the earth will visit us here, while the wicked and ungodly will envy us our comfortable homes and possessions. Take courage, brethren. I can stand in my door and can see where there is untold millions of the rich treasures of the earth — gold and silver. But the time has not come for the Saints to dig gold. It is our duty first to develop the agricultural resources of the country, for there is no country on the earth that is more productive than this. We have the finest climate, the best water, and the purest air that can be found on earth; there is no healthier climate anywhere. As for gold and silver, and the rich minerals of the earth, there is no other country that equals this; but let them alone; let others seek them, and we will cultivate the soil; for if the mines are opened first, we are a thousand miles from any base of supplies and the people would rush in here in such great numbers that they would breed a famine; and gold would not do us or them any good if there were no provisions in the land. People would starve to death with barrels of gold; they would be willing to give a barrel of gold for a barrel of flour rather than starve to death. Then, brethren, plow your land and sow wheat, plant your potatoes; let the mines alone until the time comes for you to hunt gold, though I do not think this people ever will become a mining people. It is our duty to preach the gospel, gather Israel, pay our tithing, and build temples. The worst fear that I have about this people is that they will get rich in this country, forget God and his people, wax fat, and kick themselves out of the Church and go to hell. This people will stand mobbing, robbing, poverty, and all manner of persecution, and be true. But my greater fear for them is that they cannot stand wealth; and yet they have to be tried with riches, for they will become the richest people on this earth.'" (Autobiography of James Brown, pp. 119-123)

With inspiration and fearless good leadership, Brigham Young thus persuaded the Saints to forget the gold fields and to set about establishing hundreds of small settlements throughout what they chose to call *Deseret*. Soon these settlements appeared in the areas now called Utah Valley, Ogden, Cache Valley, Sanpete Valley, etc.

The struggle and hardships experienced by the Saints did not discourage them in their missionary activities. Hundreds of the young men of the Church were sent throughout the world to carry the message of the Book of Mormon and the restoration of the Gospel to seekers of truth. Converts came by the thousands to live in Zion. The immigration was continual across the plains. In 1856 a new system of travel for many of these immigrating Saints was inaugurated. Handcart companies were organized because the handcart was much less expensive than a team of oxen or horses. These handcarts were constructed with a handle at both front and rear and could carry several hundred pounds of supplies. Thus some could push and some could pull.

Hundreds of Saints crossed the plains in this manner in safety. There were two companies, however, that experienced tragedy in their journey. The Martin and Willie companies left Winter Quarters too late in the summer, and they encountered an early winter in Wyoming, where hundreds perished before relief from the Salt Lake Valley could reach them.

"Moroni's Challenge"

And when ye shall receive these things, I would exhort you that ye would ask God, the Eternal Father, in the name of Christ, if these things are not true; and if ye shall ask with a sincere heart, with real intent, having faith in Christ, he will manifest the truth of it unto you, by the power of the Holy Ghost. Moroni 10:4.

Portraits in Words

By Joseph N. Revill

"Precepts to live by!" — not from Alma, as such.

"Now I would that ye should see that they brought upon themselves the curse; and even so doth every man that is cursed bring upon himself his own condemnation." (Alma 3:19)

Men are too often guilty of applying the thoughts of this precept to physical, visible things. Men are capable of condemning themselves to a spiritual or mental cursing as well, and then they wonder why they have lost contact with the Spirit when they find themselves in darkness.

History is replete with examples, both singular and collective, that point up the truth of this quoted precept. Alma was very aware of this condition among his people. Having had the personal experience of following an evil or unrighteous course in his early life, he found through repentance the way back into spiritual light, joy, and satisfaction. He repeatedly warned the members of the Church against false pride and vain desires: ". . . and beheld with great sorrow that the people of the church began to be lifted up in the pride of their eyes, and upon the vain things of the world, that they began to be scornful, one towards another, and they began to persecute those that did not believe according to their own will and pleasure." (Alma 4:8)

The early history of Mormonism has numerous examples from which we can and should benefit if we heed the admonition of the precept.

Oliver Cowdery was a brilliant scholar and in his early life enjoyed some choice experiences. He was privileged to have John the Baptist lay his hands on his head and ordain him, along with the Prophet Joseph Smith, to the Aaronic Priesthood. He, too, received the visitation of Peter, James, and John, witnessed as one of three, the plates of Mormon and saw Moroni, the angelic being. He was privileged to see the Savior Jesus Christ personally in the Kirtland Temple. Many other choice experiences which were his did not keep him from making the mistakes which led to his excommunication from the Church. He fell out of touch with the Spirit, contributed to the persecution of the Saints, became scornful of those in authority, and questioned their right to govern the kingdom of God.

For some ten years Oliver Cowdery was outside the Church. He experienced the buffetings of Satan, and he learned humility and appreciation for his lost blessings through personal suffering. In October, 1848, Oliver attended a conference of the Church at Kanesville, Iowa, and spoke to the assembled Saints:

> "Friends and Brethren: My name is Cowdery, Oliver Cowdery. In the early history of this Church I stood identified with her, and one in her councils. True it is that the gifts and callings of God are without repentance; not because I was better than the rest of mankind was I called; but, to fulfill the purposes of God, he called me to a high and holy calling.

"I wrote with my own pen the entire Book of Mormon (save a few pages) as it fell from the lips of the Prophet Joseph Smith, as he translated it by the gift and power of God, by means of the Urim and Thummim, or as it is called by that book, 'holy interpreters.' I beheld with my eyes, and handled with my hands the gold plates from which it was transcribed. I also saw with my eyes and handled with my hands the 'holy interpreters.' That book is true. Sidney Rigdon did not write it. Mr. Spaulding did not write it. I wrote it myself as it fell from the lips of the Prophet. It contains the everlasting Gospel, and came forth to the children of men in fulfillment of the revelations of John, where he says he saw an angel come with the everlasting Gospel to preach to every nation, kindred, tongue and people. It contains principles of salvation; and if you, my hearers, will walk by its light and obey its precepts, you will be saved with an everlasting salvation in the kingdom of God on high.

". . . I was present with Joseph when an holy angel from God came down from heaven and conferred on us, or restored the lesser or Aaronic Priesthood, and said to us at the same time, that it should remain upon the earth while the earth stands.

"I was also present with Joseph when the higher or Melchizedek Priesthood was conferred by holy angels from on high. This Priesthood we then conferred on each other, by the will and commandment of God. This Priesthood, as was then declared, is also to remain upon the earth until the last remnant of time . . ." (Essentials of Church History, p. 469)

A few days after this conference, Oliver Cowdery went to the high council at Kanesville and said:

"Brethren, for a number of years I have been separated from you. I now desire to come back. I wish to come humbly and to be one in your midst. I seek no station. I only wish to be identified with you. I am out of the Church. I am not a member of the Church, but I wish to become a member of it. I wish to come in at the door. I know the door. I have not come here to seek precedence; I come humbly, and throw myself upon the decisions of this body, knowing, as I do, that its decisions are right, and should be obeyed." (Essentials of Church History, p. 470)

True repentance, a contrite spirit, and real humility had thus prevailed in Oliver Cowdery's life. He had been the second Elder in the Church. He brought upon himself his own condemnation and his own suffering; but by his complete change of heart and sincere repentance, his sins were forgiven him, and he found his way back into the kingdom.

We can learn much and benefit greatly from the lessons of Alma's precept.

GIDEON

AMLICI

NEHOR

ALMA THE YOUNGER

Important
In This

Characters
Volume

AMULEK

ZEEZROM

ZORAM

CHIEF JUDGE

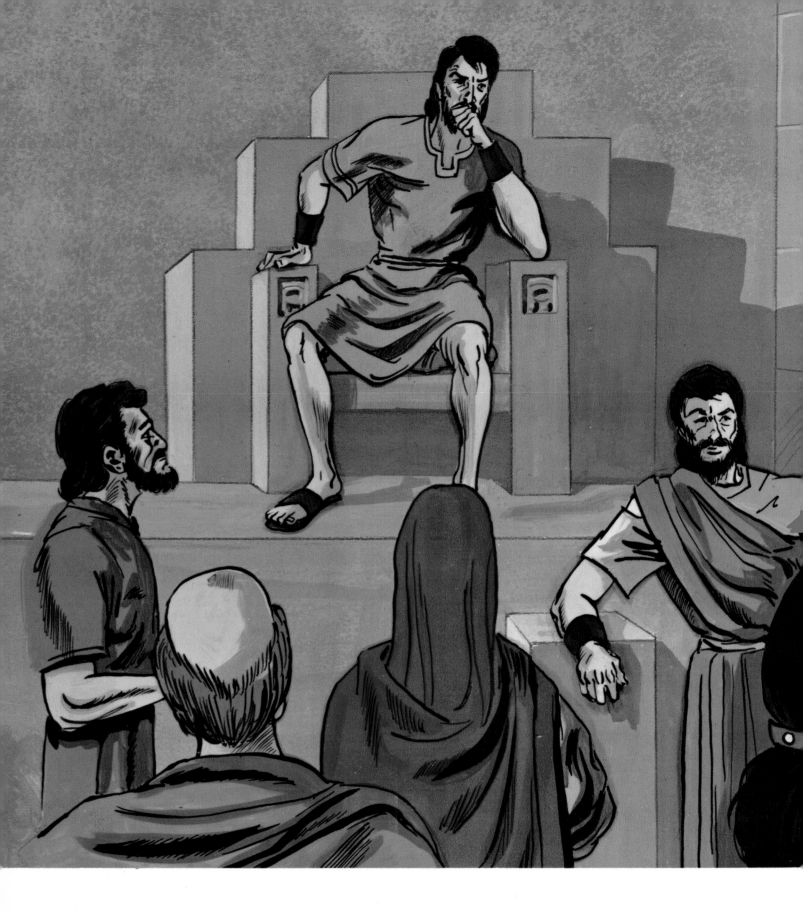

AFTER the death of the splendid and righteous king Mosiah, Alma became the first chief judge over the people of Nephi, for it had been determined that they should be ruled according to law, and especially the law of God.

A man noted for his size and strength came before Alma. His name was Nehor. He had gone among the people preaching what he thought to be the word of God,

but he was against the Church! He said that the priests and teachers should become popular and not work with their hands, that the people should support them. Moreover, he said that everyone would be saved and that the people did not need to fear and tremble. For he said that the Lord had created all men and would redeem them, and that they would have eternal life.

See Alma 1:1-4

SO many people believed Nehor that they began to support him and give him money. He began to think that he was a great man, and he began wearing expensive clothing. Then he established his own church!

One day when he was on his way to preach to his church, he began arguing with an aged teacher of the church of God, in order to get more members. But the

teacher stood his ground and challenged him with the words of God. His name was Gideon, the Gideon who, as an instrument in the hands of the Lord, helped deliver the people of Limhi out of slavery to the Lamanites! Nehor got so angry that he struck the unarmed and aged Gideon with his sword and killed him.

See Alma 1:5-9

THE people of the Church took Nehor before Alma to be judged for his crimes. Nehor pleaded his case boldly. But Alma replied: "Nehor this is the first time that priestcraft has been introduced among this people. Not only are you guilty of it, but you have tried to force it upon the people by violence—by the sword! Priestcraft would destroy our people!

You have shed the blood of a righteous man who has done much good among the people. If we let you go unpunished, his blood would come upon us for vengeance. So you are condemned to die, and this judgment is according to the law which was given by Mosiah, our last king. The people have acknowledged and support this law, and so this people must live according to it.

See Alma 1:10-14

THE people took Nehor and carried him to the top of the hill Manti, where he confessed that what he had taught was contrary to the word of God. Nehor was put to death, but despite this fact priestcraft spread throughout the land. Many of the people who loved the vain things of the world accepted it and began preaching false doctrines to get riches and honors.

But for fear of the law they did not lie openly, for liars were punished. So they pretended to teach what they believed, for the law could not punish anyone for his belief. For fear of the law they did not rob or murder. They knew that murderers were put to death and that robbers were severely punished. But the spirit of robbery and murder was in their hearts.

See Alma 1:15-18

THOSE who did not belong to the Church of God began to persecute those who did. The reason that the persecutions began was that the members of the Church were humble and preached the gospel to one another without expecting or getting any kind of material reward or payment. There was a law among them that they themselves would not persecute those who were not members and that they would never persecute each other. Nevertheless, some were proud, and so they began to argue and fight with their adversaries.

See Alma 1:19-22

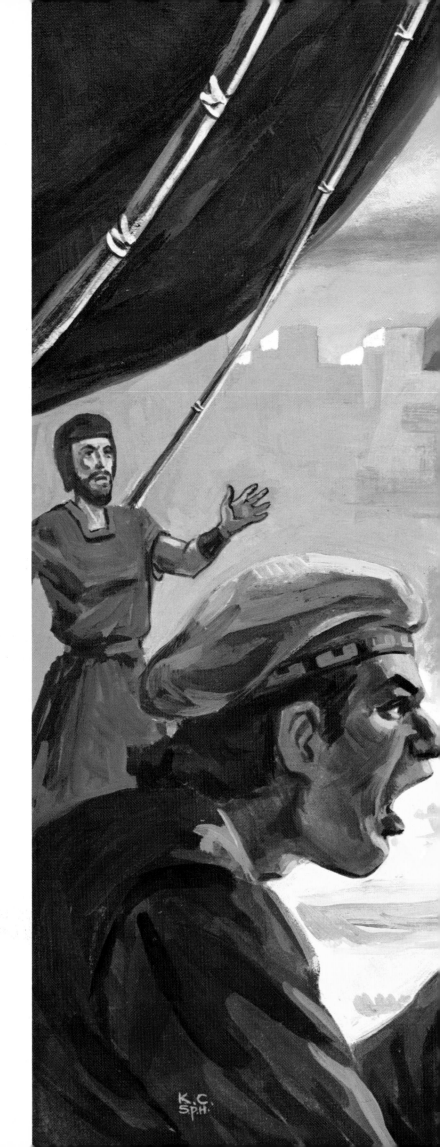

THESE persecutions caused much trouble and affliction to the Church. Many people so hardened their hearts that their names were blotted out on the records of the Church, and the members no longer remembered them. Some people withdrew from the Church of their own accord. But the members, though severely troubled and persecuted remained steadfast in their faith and in keeping the commandments of God.

When the priests stopped working to preach the gospel, the people stopped working to hear them. They worked together and worshipped together, and they were one people. No one thought he was better than his neighbor, and everyone did what he could, according to his strength and abilities to reach religious, cultural, and social goals. Everyone had equal opportunity.

See Alma 1:23-26

IF a member of the Church was in need of something, or sick, or poor, or afflicted, his brethren would give him help. The members of the Church were deeply concerned about everyone's welfare. They lived in peace despite the persecutions. They were good-looking, sensible, and moderate in their dress. Because the Church was steady and righteous in every way, it began to be very rich. There was plenty of everything that was needed—flocks, herds, fatlings of every kind, grain, gold, silver, silk, fine-twined linen, good homely cloth, and many

precious things! But they used these things only to satisfy their own basic needs and to help anyone who was in want. They clothed the naked, fed the hungry, administered to the sick. They were kind and fair to everyone—the old and the young, the enslaved and the free, both in and out of the Church. They did not love their riches but used them to help their fellow men. So they became far more wealthy than those who did not belong to the Church.

See Alma 1:27-31

THOSE not in the Church became strange and superstitious. They devoted themselves to sorcery, idleness, gossip, envy, arguing, and fighting. They wore expensive clothing, and thought that they were very important. They became liars, thieves, robbers, murderers, adulterers, and were wicked in every imaginable way. However, crime and wickedness were punished as much as possible under the law. The people became generally more peaceful, even though some crimes were committed in secret, as the fifth year of the reign of the judges came to an end.

See Alma 1:32-33

IN this same year trouble began among the people. Amlici, a cunning and wise man in the ways of the world and very much like Nehor, who had killed Gideon, got many people to accept him as their leader. They became powerful and wanted Amlici to be a king over the people. This alarmed the members of the Church and the non-members who did not follow Amlici. The law said that such a thing had to be approved by the majority of the people. If Amlici could get this majority, he would destroy the rights and freedoms of the people and the Church itself! This was the real reason that he wanted power.

So the people came together from all parts of the land, divided themselves into two groups, each man deciding whether he was for or against Amlici, and began to debate about what should happen.

See Alma 2:1-5

33

HEY voted, and gave the results to the judges. Amlici lost, and so he did not become king over the people. The people who were against Amlici were happy, but Amlici encouraged his followers to hate those who had voted against him.

See Alma 2:6-8

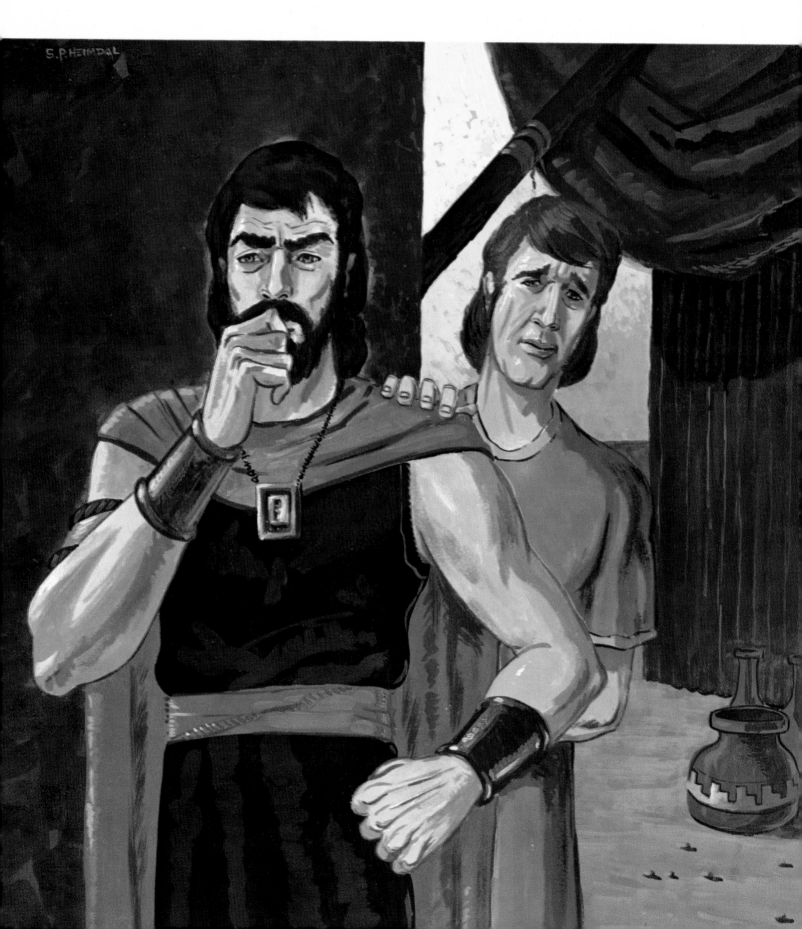

THE followers of Amlici gathered together and in spite of the voice of the people made Amlici their king. He then commanded his people, who were now called Amlicites to begin a civil war against all the others who were called Nephites. Amlici wanted to force the Nephites to accept him as their king!

See Alma 2:9-11

THE Nephites, however, knew what was happening, and so prepared to defend themselves. They armed themselves with swords, cimeters, bows and arrows, slings and stones, and many other weapons of war, and they organized themselves into military units, with captains, higher captains, and chief captains, according to the size of the units. Amlici did the same thing, and appointed rulers and leaders to lead his people into battle.

See Alma 2:12-14

THE Amlicites went to the hill Amnihu, east of the river Sidon, which ran by the land of Zarahemla, and began to fight the Nephites. As chief judge and governor of the Nephites, Alma led his army against the Amlicites. There was a great battle in which many Nephites were killed, but the Lord strengthened the Nephites, and they killed even more Amlicites. The Amlicites retreated, the Nephites pursuing them all day and killing even more,—in all, 12,532, as against 6,562 slain Nephites.

See Alma 2:15-19

THE Nephites, after they could pursue the Amlicites no longer, pitched their tents for the night in the valley of Gideon which was named after the Gideon whom Nehor killed.

See Alma 2:20

LMA sent spies to see what the remnant of the Amlicites were doing. He wanted to discover their plans and strategy so that he might guard against them and preserve his people. Alma's spies were Zeram, Amnor, Manti, and Limher.

See Alma 2:21-22

ALMA'S spies returned quickly the next day, and with astonishment and fear said: "We followed the Amlicites to the land of Minon, above the land of Zarahemla in the course of the land of Nephi, and we saw a great army of Lamanites. The Amlicites have joined the Lamanites! Together, they are attacking our brethren who are fleeing before them with their wives, children, and flocks toward our city Zarahemla. If we do not go there immediately, they will capture our city, and our fathers, wives, and children will be killed."

See Alma 2:23-25

LMA and his army took their tents and quickly left the valley of Gideon and travelled toward Zarahemla. As they were crossing the river Sidon, the great army of the Lamanites and the Amlicites confronted them and tried to destroy them. But the Lord had listened to their prayers and had strengthened them.

See Alma 2:26-28

AS the Nephites began to defeat the Lamanites and Amlicites, Alma saw Amlici and they began fighting each other face to face! Alma cried out: "O Lord, have mercy and help me! I want to save my people!" As soon as Alma said these words, he killed Amlici with his sword.

Then Alma saw the king of the Lamanites and began to fight him! But the king of the Lamanites ran away and sent his guards to fight Alma. But Alma and his guards killed many of them and drove the rest back.

See Alma 2:29-33

ALMA and some of his army gained control of the west bank of the river Sidon and threw the bodies of the dead Lamanites into the water so that the rest of the Nephite army could cross the river and fight the Lamanites and Amlicites. When they had all crossed, the enemy retreated, despite their great numbers. The Lamanites and Amlicites ran into the wilderness to the west and north, beyond the borders of the land. But the Nephites caught them and killed most of them.

See Alma 2:34-36

THE Lamanites and Amlicites that were left scattered to the west and north, far beyond the borders of the land, until they reached the wilderness Hermounts, which was infested with wild and ravenous animals. Many of the Lamanites and Amlicites died of their wounds and were eaten by these animals and the vultures of the air. Their bones have been found and have been heaped up to show how many there were.

See Alma 2:37-38

48

THE Nephites buried their dead and returned to their homes and families. Many of their wives and children had been slain with the sword, and many of their flocks, herds, and fields of grain had been destroyed.

The Amlicites had marked their foreheads with red, as the Lamanites had done, but they had not shaved their heads. The Lamanites wore only loin cloths and their armor, and they carried their bows and arrows and their stones and slings and other weapons with them. And the skin of the Lamanites was dark, which was the mark of the curse upon them from their forefathers for having transgressed and rebelled against Nephi, Jacob, Joseph, and Sam, who were just and holy men! This was done so that the Lamanites could be known apart from the Nephites; the Lord wanted to preserve his people and their traditions. Anyone who joined the Lamanites became just like them, and the curse of the Lamanites was upon them.

Those who continued to believe the records and traditions that had been brought from Jerusalem were called Nephites; they lived according to the commandments of God and were his people. It is they who kept not only their own records but those of the Lamanites.

So the Amlicites, because of their disbelief and rebellion, became Lamanites. They brought the curse upon them themselves! And so it is that if ever a man is condemned in God's eyes, he brings the condemnation on himself through his own choice.

The hearts of the Lamanites were so hard that even though Alma and his army had won a great and decisive victory the Lamanites organized another army and came to fight the Nephites in the same place.

See Alma 3:1-20

LMA sent a great army against the Lamanites, but, because he had been wounded, he did not go himself. The Nephites killed many of the Lamanites and drove the rest out of the land. Then they returned home and established peace and for a time they were no longer troubled by their enemies.

So ended the fifth year of the reign of the judges. In one year tens of thousands had died in the war, and they went to the eternal world to be judged for their deeds, whether good or evil, according to the spirit of prophecy.

See Alma 3:21-27

IN the sixth year of the reign of the judges the land of Zarahemla was peaceful, but the people suffered because so many had been lost in the war with the Amlicites and Lamanites. And they had lost many of their animals, crops, and belongings. Everyone mourned, and they thought that the judgment of God had been sent upon them for their wickedness. They knew what they had to do. They established the Church more fully, and many were baptized by Alma in the waters of Sidon. In the seventh year 3500 joined the Church through the waters of baptism!

See Alma 4:1-5

IN the eighth year the members of the Church became proud because they were rich and expensively dressed, and because they could satisfy themselves so easily through their industry. Alma and the priests and teachers he had consecrated were very sorry to see this happen, for it meant that the people were becoming wicked again. They became vain, scornful, pleasure-seekers, and they began to persecute each other for not conforming to the many false values and customs that they themselves had created. The members of the Church became envious, malicious, and so filled with pride that they were more wicked than the non-members! Amazingly enough, the wickedness of the people of the Church was a great stumbling block to those who did not belong to the Church. So the Church began to fail in its progress.

Then in the ninth year the wickedness of the people in and out of the Church prepared them for their destruction. There was great inequality, some full of pride, others full of hate for their brethren, and others ignoring or reviling the sick, hungry, and needy. But there was great sorrow among the righteous. They did what they could to save the people by doing righteous things, by acting according to the spirit of prophecy, and by suffering all kinds of persecutions for Christ's sake. They knew that the coming sacrifice of Christ for the sins of all mankind would begin the resurrection of the dead!

Although Alma was sorrowful because of the wickedness of the people, the Spirit of the Lord did not fail him.

See Alma 4:6-15

ALMA chose a wise man from among the elders of the Church and gave him power to represent the people in enacting laws according to the laws they had already received. Alma also gave him power to enforce all the laws. So this man, whose name was Nephihah, received part of Alma's authority; so Alma appointed him chief judge so that he could judge and govern the people. But Alma kept his office as high priest of the Church so that he could go among his people, the Nephites, to preach the word of God and to get them to remember their promises and duty to God. He tried to destroy their wickedness by directly describing it to them and by bearing his testimony to them. Alma gave his full time to this effort.

See Alma 4:16-20

ALMA preached to the people in the land of Zarahemla and then throughout the land. This is what he said in Zarahemla: "I, Alma, am the high priest called to lead the Church, and I have this authority from God. My father, Alma, established this Church in the land of Mormon, where he baptized his brethren in the waters of Mormon. He and his people were delivered from the wicked king Noah by the mercy and power of God. After that, the Lamanites enslaved them in the wilderness. But again the Lord rescued them and brought them to this land so that the Church could grow.

"Do you remember these things? Do you remember God's mercy? Do you remember that God has delivered our people from hell? They were in the midst of darkness, and the Lord gave us the light of his word. They were not destroyed! Instead, the bands of death about them were loosed, and they sang of the Lord's redeeming love!

"My father, Alma, believed the prophecies of Abinadi, who was a holy prophet. Alma preached to your fathers; they believed him, and put their trust in God, and endured to the end. They were saved!

"What are you compared to them? Do you acknowledge that God created you? What would you say if he called you before him now? Do you think you can lie to him when that time comes, as it surely will?

"You will remember every detail of your wickedness when you confess what you are to him. And you know that you cannot be saved unless you are purified of your sins.

"Can you sing a song of the Lord's redeeming love? Can you make yourselves what he wants you to be?

"Have you given up your false pride? Have you become humble? You must prepare to meet your God quickly, for the kingdom of Heaven awaits you sooner than you know, for it is at hand.

"Follow the commandments of God in every detail, remembering that good works are the expression of the mind and spirit that is full of faith and humility. Do not be proud of the things of this world.

"The Lord calls to you to come unto him as sheep come to the good shepherd. If you are not of his fold, to whom do you belong? Do you belong to the devil? If you say that you do not belong to the Lord, you are liars, and liars belong to the devil.

"You know that whatever is good comes from God and that evil comes from the devil. Are your works good or evil?

"I speak to you with the energy of my whole soul because God has commanded me to tell you these things! I know they are true! The Holy Spirit made them known to me!

"Jesus Christ will surely come to take away the sins of the world, of every man who believes steadfastly in his name. Repent, oh people of the earth! The king of heaven and earth is coming to establish his kingdom here!

"My brethren, do not trample on the words of God. You are all his children, and in that sense equal before him. So do not persecute your brethren in the Church who are doing God's will. Be righteous so that you can be numbered among them."

See Alma 5:1-62

ALMA finished speaking. Many repented, and their faith in God enabled Alma to begin building up the Church again. He ordained priests and elders by the laying on of hands, and many were baptized who were not members. The members who did not repent were excommunicated. The reform movement in the Church had begun in Zarahemla!

Alma then left the city of Zarahemla and went east of the river Sidon into the valley of Gideon, which was named after the Gideon who was slain by Nehor. Alma began preaching to the members of the Church there according to the spirit of prophecy. He preached the principle of redemption and the divinity of Christ in the spirit of the holy priesthood which he held.

He said: "My brethren, because I have given my political power to another, I can now come to you and preach the gospel with more time and freedom. I hope that you have not fallen into sin as have your brethren in Zarahemla. But they have repented and have become righteous again.

"Maintain your righteousness, my brethren, for the Lord will come soon!" Then Alma told the people of Gideon about the life and mission of the Savior, how he would redeem men from their sins through his personal sacrifice on the cross and how he would conquer death!

Alma said: "My brethren I know that you believe in the principles of the gospel; so my joy is great. You have not fallen away. But let me nevertheless remind you of your duty to God so that you may walk blameless before him. Be humble, submissive, gentle, patient, moderate; be diligent in keeping the Lord's commandments. Have faith, hope, and charity. This is my testimony to you. May the peace of God be with you and with your families and everything that you possess. Amen."

See Alma 6:1-8; 7:1-27

ALMA returned to his home in Zarahemla after his work in the service of the Lord.

The ninth year of the reign of the judges ended and the tenth began.

Alma, after a long rest, continued his holy work. He went to the land of Melek, on the west of the river Sidon, on the west by the borders of the wilderness. He preached the gospel to the people in the righteousness of his priesthood. Many came to him and were baptized.

See Alma 8:1-5

HEN he finished his work in Melek, Alma went north to a city named Ammonihah, after the man who first possessed the land, and began preaching the word of God to the people. Satan had gained control of their hearts; so they would not listen to Alma. However, Alma prayed mightily that God would pour out his spirit on them and that they would repent and be baptized. But the people said to him: "We know who you are. You are Alma, the high priest of the church that you have established in many parts of the land, according to your traditions. We do not belong to your church, and we think that your traditions are foolish. You have no power over us. Nephihah is the chief judge!" Then they cursed Alma, spit on him, and threw him out of the city.

See Alma 8:6-13

LMA continued his journey to a city called Aaron. He was very sad because the people of Ammonihah were so wicked and would not repent.

An angel appeared to him, saying: "You are blessed, Alma; so rejoice. You have been faithful in keeping the commandments of God from the time you first received a message from him. I brought it to you.

"Alma, return to the city of Ammonihah and preach to the people. Tell them to repent, or God will destroy them. Even now there is a conspiracy among them to destroy their liberty, which was established according to the will of the Lord."

See Alma 8:13-17

ALMA returned to Ammonihah speedily, entering the city from another way—the south. He was hungry and asked a man he saw to give him some food, identifying himself as a humble servant of God. The man said: "I am a Nephite, and I know you are a holy prophet of God. An angel came to me in a vision and said that you would come. Come to my house and I will feed you. Your presence will be a blessing to me and my house!"

See Alma 8:18-20

ALMA learned that the man's name was Amulek. They went to Amulek's house, where Amulek fed Alma. When Alma finished eating, he blessed Amulek and his house and gave thanks to God. Then he said: "I am Alma, the high priest over the land, and I have been called to preach the word of God according to the spirit of revelation and prophecy. When I preached here in Ammonihah, the people rejected me and cast me out. I thought that I would never come back. But the Lord wants me to try again."

Alma rested in Amulek's home many days before he began preaching again.

See Alma 8:21-27

BUT Alma saw that the people of Ammonihah were becoming even more wicked. It was revealed to Alma that he should tell Amulek to call his people to repentance to avoid the anger of God. So Amulek joined Alma in preaching to the people, and both were filled with the Holy Ghost.

So great was their spirituality that they could not be confined in dungeons or even killed, and these things they demonstrated to show the power of the Lord in them.

This is what Alma said: "God has commanded Amulek and me to preach to you, the people of Ammonihah. But you question my prophecy that the earth and this city will pass away." But the people did not know that his prophecy was true. They even questioned that God would send them just one man to prophesy such important events. They were just about to seize him, but they discovered they could not.

Alma said: "Remember the prophecies of father Lehi, who came from Jerusalem? Only if you are righteous will you prosper in this land. The Lamanites, who have received falsehoods from their fathers, will receive more mercy than you, to whom the truth is near at hand. Someday they will be taught what you reject and will receive the true traditions.

"The Lamanites will come upon you suddenly and destroy you if you do not repent. God will not let you live in your wickedness. You have received so many blessings, and the Lord has answered your righteous prayers. You have been so highly favored! No wonder the Lord will not let you remain wicked! He has sent an angel to visit many of his people, who has instructed them to go among the people and preach the gospel and call you to repentance. The Lord is coming! All people will be judged according to what they create and what they do. Be and do what the Lord wants you to be and do, and begin now!"

But the people had hardened their hearts and would not listen to Alma. They tried to seize him and put him into prison, but the Lord would not let them.

See Alma 8:28-32; 9:1-33

64

MULEK stepped forward and also began preaching to the people of Ammonihah. This is part of what Amulek said: "I am Amulek, the son of Giddonah, who was the son of Ishmael, who was a descendant of the Aminadi who interpreted the writing on the wall of the temple, which was written by the finger of God. Aminadi was a descendant of Nephi, the son of Lehi, who left Jerusalem. Lehi was a descendant of Manasseh, who was the son of Joseph, who was sold into Egypt by his brothers.

"So, my brethren, I have many relatives and friends among you; I think I have your good will. I have worked hard for my living and for my possessions.

"However, I have never known very much about the ways of the Lord, and about his mysteries and marvellous power. But I know now that I was at a disadvantage, for I have seen the Lord's will among us, working for the preservation of his people.

"Once my heart was hard, and I rebelled against God until the fourth day of the seventh month of the tenth year of the reign of the judges. I was journeying at that time to see some close relatives when an angel of the Lord appeared to me and said: 'Amulek, return home. A prophet of the eternal God is there, whom you must feed. This man has tried hard to save the people. He is hungry after fasting for the people, and if you help and feed him he will bless your home, and so will the Lord.'"

Amulek continued: "I obeyed the angel, and, on the way home, I met Alma, and I knew instantly that he is a holy man and testifies of the truth. I fed him, and indeed, he has blessed my home. The spirit of God is with him. You should listen to him and believe him."

The people were astonished to hear Amulek say these things, because now there was another witness to their wickedness and guilt and to the truth of Alma's prophecies about the coming of the Lord.

But some lawyers wanted to question Alma and Amulek in order to catch them with their own words, condemn them by the law, and put them into prison or execute them. The lawyers were trained in such evil cunning. They began to question Amulek, but they could not know that Amulek knew what they were trying to do.

Amulek said: "You are a wicked and perverse generation, for I know that you work with the devil to lay traps and snares to catch the holy ones of God. You try to pervert the righteous, but you are bringing down the wrath of God on your heads, even to the destruction of this people. Mosiah, our last king, prophesied what would happen to you if you could not govern yourselves, and you became evil. Repent before it is too late! The kingdom of heaven is at hand.

"You would be destroyed right now were it not for the righteous in the land. Their prayers have saved you! If you reject them and make them leave your land, the fierce anger of the Lord will come upon you instantly! You will suffer from famine, pestilence, and war!"

See Alma 9:34; 10:1-23

THE people became angry with Amulek. They cried out: "This man reviles our laws and our lawyers, whom we have chosen!"

But Amulek said: "Satan has a hold on your hearts! He blinds you to the truth! I have not spoken against your laws, but in favor of them, to your condemnation. Your lawyers and judges are causing your destruction!"

The people said: "Now we know that this man is a child of the devil, for he

has lied to us. He has spoken against our law, and now says that he has not. He has reviled our lawyers and judges."

The lawyers promised themselves to remember Amulek's words so that they would be ready at any time to condemn him. Their leader in accusing Alma and Amulek was Zeezrom, an expert in the affairs of the people. Like the other lawyers, he was interested only in getting gain.

See Alma 10:24-32

ZEEZROM questioned Amulek. An expert in the ways of the devil, he asked: "Will you answer my questions?"
Amulek answered: "Yes, if they are according to the Spirit of the Lord."
Zeezrom replied: "Here are six onties of silver. I will give them to you if you deny the existence of a Supreme Being."

See Alma 11:21-22

AMULEK said: "You child of hell, why do you tempt me? Did you not know that the righteous do not yield to such temptations? Do you believe that there is no God? You know that God lives, but you love money more than him.

"You have lied to me before God. You said: 'Here are six onties of silver. I will give them to you if you deny the existence of a Supreme Being!' But in your heart you know that you would keep them from me. All you wanted me to do was to deny God so that you would have a reason to kill me. For this evil you shall get the reward you deserve."

See Alma 11:23-25

ZEEZROM replied: "You say that there is a true and living God?"
Amulek said: "Yes."
Zeezrom said: "Is there more than one God?"
Amulek said: "No."
Zeezrom continued: "How do you know?"
Amulek replied: "An angel told me."

See Alma 11:26-31

ZEEZROM said again: "Will the Son of God come?"
Amulek said: "Yes."
Zeezrom replied: "Shall he save his people in their sins?"
Amulek answered: "He shall not, for it is impossible for him to deny his word."

See Alma 11:32-34

73

ZEEZROM said to the people: "Remember what Amulek has said. He said that there is one God, and now he says that the Son of God will come, but not to save his people. Amulek thinks he has the authority to command God."

Amulek replied: "Zeezrom, you have lied. For you say I spoke as if I had authority to command God because I said that he will not save his people in their sins. God has said that no unclean thing can inherit the kingdom of heaven."

Zeezrom said: "Is the Son of God the very Eternal Father of heaven and of earth?"

Amulek replied: "Yes, he is the very Eternal Father of heaven and earth, and of all things that are in them. He is the beginning and end, the first and the last. He shall come into the world to redeem his people, and he shall take upon him the transgressions of those who believe on his name, that they might have eternal life, for salvation will come to none else. The wicked will be as they were, except that the bands of death will be loosed. The day will come when all shall rise from the dead and stand before God and be judged according to their works. The death of Christ will loose the bands of temporal death. The spirit and the body will be reunited in its perfect form, as a soul, much as we are now, and we shall be brought to stand before God, knowing as we do now, having a bright recollection of our guilt. This restoration will come to everyone, and not a hair of the head will be lost. The mortal body will become an immortal body and will die no more, and never again will the spirit and the body be separated, and there will be no more corruption."

See Alma 11:35-45

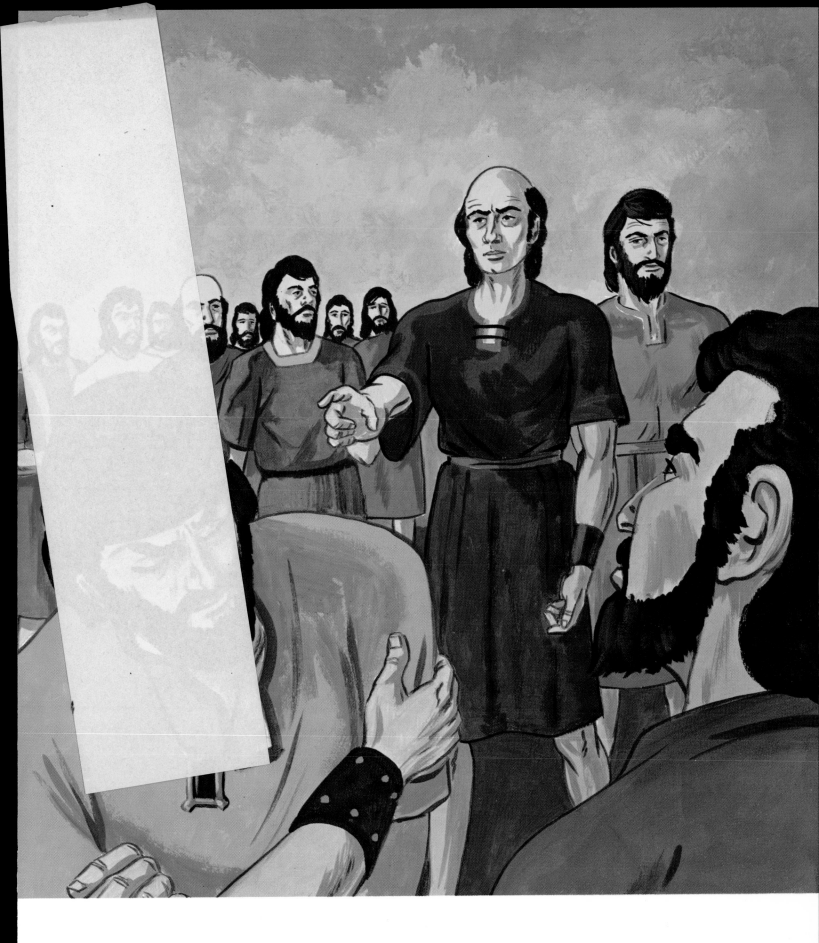

WHEN Amulek finished speaking, the people marvelled and Zeezrom trembled.

See Alma 11:46

ALMA saw that Amulek had silenced Zeezrom, for Amulek had caught Zeezrom lying in his attempt to destroy Amulek. Zeezrom trembled because he was guilty. Alma told Zeezrom even more of the truth of the gospel. The people gathered around them to hear Alma.

Alma said: "Zeezrom, now you know in your heart that you have lied to man and to God. God knows all your thoughts, and the Spirit of God has shown them to us. Your plan was clever, like the devil's. The devil has caught you in his snare. He wants to catch this people through you. He wants to bring you all down into hell to be bound in his chains forever."

Zeezrom was convinced of the power of God and began to tremble even more. And he knew that Alma and Amulek knew his innermost thoughts.

See Alma 12:1-7

ZEEZROM asked Alma and Amulek more about the kingdom of God. He said to Alma: "What does Amulek mean about the resurrection of the dead—that all shall rise from the dead, both the just and the unjust, and be brought before God to be judged according to their works?"

Alma replied: "Many know the mysteries of God, but the mysteries are revealed only according to the ability of the people to receive them. It is harder for those who have not fully accepted God to understand, and so they fall under Satan's influence more easily. Those who have not accepted God fully are in danger of losing what truth they have! Without the saving truth, men are in danger of destruction!

"Amulek has spoken plainly about death, about being raised from mortality to immortality, and about God's judgment. Our works will save or condemn us as will our very thoughts! At the time of the judgment we will realize that God is fair and just and that he is kind and merciful. He can save every man who believes in him and repents.

"For a second death will follow the first death for those who die in their sins. This is a spiritual death, which concerns the loss of a knowledge of righteousness. The torments will lie like a lake of fire and brimstone, whose flames last forever. Satan will have complete mastery over those who do not repent. It will be as if Christ had not offered them redemption. They cannot be redeemed according to God's justice; and they cannot die into a deeper corruption. And they know that they will have brought all this upon themselves."

See Alma 12:8-18

HE people were even more astonished when Alma finished speaking. Antionah, a chief ruler among them, came forward and said to Alma: "Do you mean that men can become immortal and never die? And what does the scripture mean when it says that God placed guardian angels and a flaming sword on the east of Eden to keep our first parents out lest they enter and eat the fruit of the tree of life, and live forever?"

Alma replied: "I was about to explain this matter. Adam fell because he ate the forbidden fruit, and so man became lost and fallen. If Adam had then eaten the fruit of the tree of life, there would have been no death, and the word would have been void, making God a liar, for he said, 'If you eat, you will surely die.'

"The temporal death comes to all men. But they can repent in this life and prepare to meet God after the resurrection of the dead. Without the plan of redemption there could have been no resurrection. But there is a plan of redemption!

"If Adam and Eve had eaten of the fruit of the tree of life, they would have been miserable forever, without the plan of redemption to come to God. But it was necessary that man should die and be judged. So he sent angels to talk with man and show them God's glory, if they would only believe in him and do holy works. Then God could help them avoid the second, or spiritual, death. Only in Christ can men be saved. My brethren, believe in him! Repent and be saved!"

See Alma 12:19-37

REMEMBER God gave his children the commandments by which they can be saved. And he ordained priests, after his holy order, to teach them the ways of the Son of God. This is the Melchizedek Priesthood. It is given to those who have proved themselves worthy of it from the foundation of the world. Those who possess it and honor it will be high priests forever, their garments being washed white by the blood of the Lamb. Melchizedek himself was a great example to all as a high priest. He was a righteous king, a great missionary and a reformer."

When Alma finished, he stretched out his hand to the people and cried out in a mighty voice, "The voice of the Lord, through his angels, declares this truth to all nations. He declares it to us, in this distant place. Let all men rejoice! We know that the Lord is coming. The words of our fathers will be fulfilled in the spirit of prophecy. Please listen to me and humble yourselves before the Lord. Pray continually to him that you will not be tempted more than you can bear. Have faith. Be meek, patient, and full of love, and you will be lifted up in your love of God at the last day."

See Alma 13:1-31

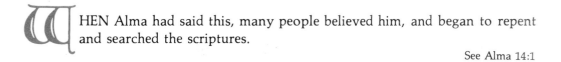

HEN Alma had said this, many people believed him, and began to repent and searched the scriptures.

See Alma 14:1

BUT most of them wanted to kill Alma and Amulek. They were angry because Alma spoke so plainly and understandably to Zeezrom and because, they said, Amulek had lied to them, reviled their law, lawyers, and judges, and had accused them of being wicked.

See Alma 14:2-3

UT these wicked people could not kill Alma and Amulek, but they did bind them with strong cords and take them before the chief judge of the land.

See Alma 14:4

THESE people went to the chief judge to testify against Alma and Amulek, accusing them of saying that there was but one God and that he would send his son among the people, but that his son would not save them!

See Alma 14:5

ZEEZROM was astonished at the testimony against Alma and Amulek. He knew the blindness of the minds of the wicked people around him. He had caused it! He felt profoundly guilty, and he felt the pains of hell.

He cried to the people saying: "Look at me! I am the guilty one! Alma and Amulek are spotless before God. Please repent!" But they reviled him and said that the devil had possessed him.

See Alma 14:6-7

THE wicked people seized all who believed the gospel of Christ, including wives and children, and threw them and the holy scriptures into the fire. Then they took Alma and Amulek to the place of this martyrdom so that they might see what was happening.

See Alma 14:8

AMULEK suffered when he saw that the women and children were being burned to death. He said to Alma: "How can we watch this awful scene? Let us use the power of the priesthood, stretch out our hands, and save them!"

But Alma said: "The Spirit will not let me, for the Lord is receiving them into his glory. The Lord is letting the wicked condemn themselves at their own hands

so that the Lord's judgment upon them will be just. The blood of the innocent will cry out mightily against the wicked on judgment day."

Amulek replied: "Alma, they will also burn us."

Alma said: "Be it according to the will of the Lord. But our work is not finished; so they will not burn us."

WHEN the bodies of those who died in the fire, and the holy scriptures, were consumed, the chief judge of the land came to Alma and Amulek and, as they were being tied up, he struck them in the face and said to them: "You have seen what we have done! Are you going to preach to the people again that they are going to be thrown into a lake of fire and brimstone? You do not even have the power to save those whom we have just burned to death! And God has not saved them, even though they belong to your faith." The chief struck them again and said: "What do you have to say for yourselves?"

Alma and Amulek knew that this judge belonged to the order and faith of Nehor, who slew Gideon.

See Alma 14:14-16

ALMA and Amulek said nothing; so the chief judge struck them again and had the officers of the land throw them into prison.

See Alma 14:17

WHEN Alma and Amulek had been in prison three days, many lawyers, judges, priests, and teachers who accepted the false teachings of Nehor came to see them and question them. But Alma and Amulek said nothing. The judge said: "Why do you not answer us? You know we can burn you to death! Speak!" But again Alma and Amulek said nothing.

See Alma 14:18-19

ALL who had come to see and question Alma and Amulek went away, not knowing what to do. But they came back the next day and took turns striking Alma and Amulek in the face. They said: "Are you going to judge us again and condemn our law? If you are right, you must have the power to escape from us!" They said many more things, showing their malice and hatred by gritting their teeth and spitting on Alma and Amulek. They starved Alma and Amulek, did not give them any water to drink, took their clothes away from them, and kept them tied up.

Alma and Amulek suffered for many days. The chief judge over the land of Ammonihah came again with his wicked followers, struck Alma and Amulek again, and said: "If you have the power of God in you, escape from us now, and we will believe that the Lord will destroy this people, as you have said!"

And it was the twelfth day of the tenth month of the tenth year of the reign of the judges over the people of Nephi.

See Alma 14:20-24

THE chief judge and his followers again took turns striking Alma and Amulek, everyone repeating the chief judge's words. When they had finished, the power of God came upon Alma and Amulek, who then stood up.

Alma cried: "O Lord, how long will we suffer? Give us strength according to our faith in Christ so that we can break free!" Then Alma and Amulek became so strong that they broke free from the cords around them. When the people saw this, they began to run away for fear that they would be destroyed.

See Alma 14:25-26

THE people were so afraid that they fell down and could not get out of the prison. Then there was an earthquake! The earth shook mightily, and the walls of the prison broke in two and fell! The chief judge, the lawyers, priests, and teachers who had persecuted Alma and Amulek were crushed and killed under them!

100

See Alma 14:27

LMA and Amulek walked out of the prison unhurt. The Lord had given them power according to their faith in Christ. Everyone in the prison was killed but them!

They went into the city. A great many heard the great sounds of the destruction and came running to see what had happened. They saw Alma and Amulek coming out of the prison, and they saw that the prison had been completely destroyed. They were filled with fear and ran away from Alma and Amulek as if lions were chasing them!

103   See Alma 14:28-29

THE Lord commanded Alma and Amulek to leave the city. They arrived later in the land of Sidom, where they found all the people who had left the land of Ammonihah because they had been persecuted and stoned for believing the words of Alma. The people told Alma and Amulek what had happened to them and how the power of the Lord had saved them.

104

See Alma 15:1-2

ALMA and Amulek saw Zeezrom, who was very sick. He thought that Alma and Amulek had been killed and that because of his wickedness he was responsible. His mind was so disturbed that a burning fever had taken possession of him. He had thought about his sins so deeply that he felt that he could not be saved.

When Zeezrom found out that Alma and Amulek had come to the land of Sidom, he felt encouraged. He sent a message immediately to them that he would like them to visit him. Alma and Amulek came to him as soon as they received the message. They found Zeezrom very sick with the fever. Zeezrom reached out his hand to them, asking them to heal him.

Alma took him by the hand and said: "Do you believe that Christ can save mankind, and you?"

Zeezrom said: "Alma, I believe everything that you have said."

Alma replied: "If you believe that Christ can redeem mankind, you can be healed."

Zeezrom said: "Yes, I do, Alma."

Then Alma said: "O Lord, our God, have mercy on Zeezrom and heal him according to his faith in Christ."

See Alma 15:3-10

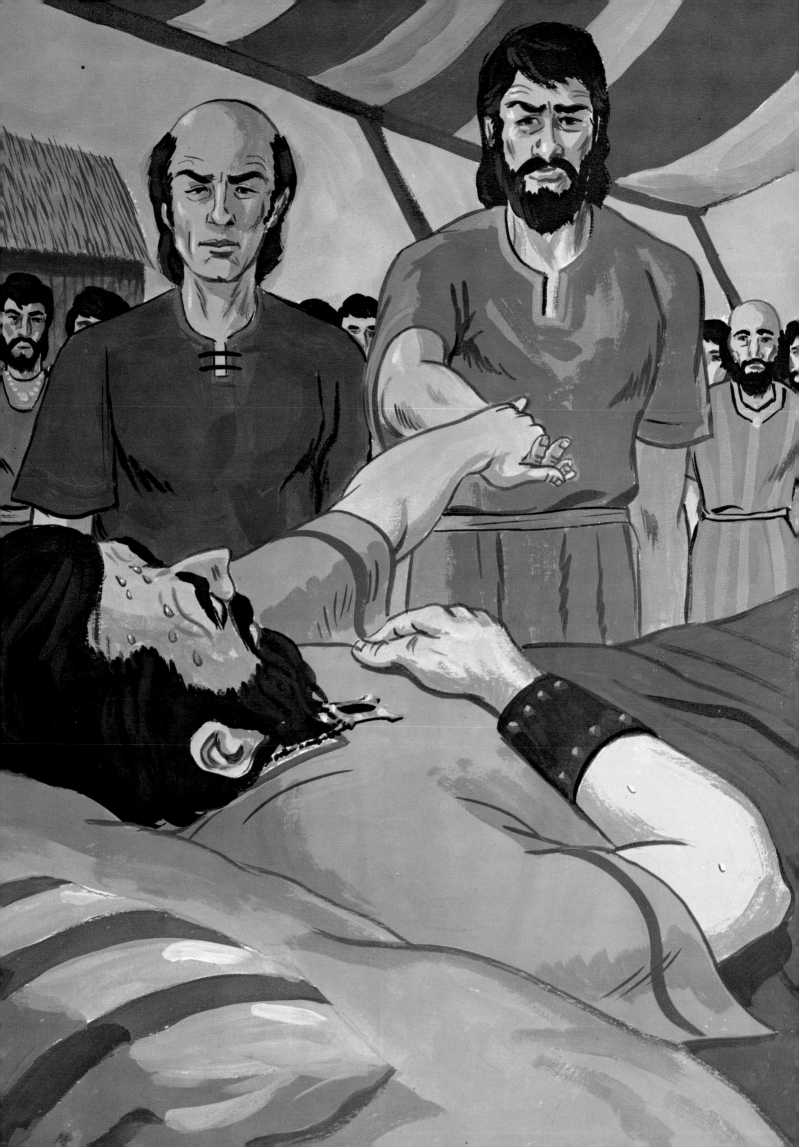

As soon as Alma said these words, Zeezrom leaped to his feet and began to walk. Everyone was amazed. The news of this marvellous happening went everywhere in the land of Sidom.

See Alma 15:11

LMA baptized Zeezrom unto the Lord, and from that time on Zeezrom preached the gospel to the people.

Alma established a church in the land of Sidom, and consecrated priests and teachers to lead the people, to do missionary work, and to baptize those who wanted to become members.

Many people wanted to be baptized, and they came from many places in the land.

But the people in the land of Ammonihah remained hard-hearted, and they did not repent of their sins; they thought that the power of Alma and Amulek came from the devil. They remained loyal to the evil doctrines of Nehor, and they did not believe in repentance from their sins.

See Alma 15:12-15

AMULEK, because he had accepted the gospel and because he had forsaken his gold, silver, and precious things, had been rejected by those who were once his friends and by his father and the rest of his relatives. So Alma, because he saw that the Church was flourishing in the land of Sidom, took Amulek to his own house in the land of Zarahemla, helped him solve his personal problems, and strengthened him in the Lord.

And so ended the tenth year of the reign of the judges over the people of Nephi.

See Alma 15:16-19

ZARAHEMLA was at peace. But on the fifth day of the second month of the eleventh year the cry of war was heard throughout the land. The Lamanites had come in from the wilderness side, on the borders of the land, into the city of Ammonihah, and had begun killing the people and destroying the city. Before the Nephites could raise a large enough army to fight them, they had killed everyone in the city, and some on the borders of Noah. They had taken others captive into the wilderness.

The Nephites wanted these to be freed.

See Alma 16:1-4

ZORAM, who was chief captain over the armies of the Nephites and his two sons, Lehi and Aha, deeply appreciated Alma's position as high priest over the Church and knew that Alma had the spirit of prophecy. They went to him and asked him whether the Lord wanted them to go into the wilderness in search of those who had been captured.

Alma inquired of the Lord. Alma returned and told them that the Lamanites would cross the river Sidon in the south wilderness, away up beyond the borders of Manti into the south wilderness, which was on the east side of the river Sidon.

See Alma 16:5-7

ZORAM led his armies into the wilderness, caught the Lamanites, scattered them, and rescued those who had been captured. Not one had been lost, and they returned to their homes and lands.

So at the end of the eleventh year all the people of Ammonihah had been destroyed, and their city also, that they said could not be destroyed because it was so great. But in one day it had been left desolate, and dogs and wild beasts of the wilderness mangled its dead.

Nevertheless, after many days the dead were heaped up and covered with a shallow covering. The stench was so bad that it was many years before the people repossessed the land. It was called the Desolation of Nehors, after the man whose doctrines led the people of Ammonihah into wickedness.

See Alma 16:8-11

FOR three years there was peace in the land. Alma and Amulek preached repentance in the temples, sanctuaries, and synagogues, which were built after the manner of the Jews. Many more had been chosen for this work, and the Church grew and flourished throughout the land.

There was no inequality among the people, and the Lord poured out his Spirit upon men that they might be prepared to receive the gospel as it would be at the time of his coming, that they might be grafted as a branch into the true vine, and that they might enter into the rest of the Lord.

115

See Alma 16:12-17

HE priests preached against wickedness of all kinds and held up the promise of the atonement of Jesus Christ, which would come. They preached that the dead would be resurrected and that Christ would appear to the people after his resurrection. The people were filled with joy at this wonderful news.

And so ended the fourteenth year of the reign of the judges over the people of Nephi.

117

See Alma 16:18-21

Pearls for Thought

—By Dr. Paul R. Cheesman

NEPHITE MONETARY SYSTEM

Because Mormon was abridging the religious history of the Nephites, it is difficult to understand why he took the time to give such a detailed account of the monetary system of Alma's time. It must be understood that a strong possibility exists that the monetary system mentioned in the Book of Mormon was not necessarily minted coins in the precise definition of "coins." The account in Alma 11 makes no mention of the actual material of the money, although the metals are identified.

It is interesting to note that the unit relationship of the Nephite exchange, 1-2-4-7, is the same relationship that is used in some modern punched cards for computer purposes.

As far as archaeology is concerned, the belief that many items were used for exchange purposes is popular. Small copper axes, fish hooks, tweezers, bells, rattles, rings, bracelets, and beans have been thought of as units of money.

By 600 B.C. the Greeks, using the plentiful gold and silver of their mines and stream beds, produced so much money that coins were plentiful. Whether or not Lehi's or Mulek's colonies used coins for money is unknown. Most numismatists subscribe to the view that coinage had its beginning in Asia Minor in about the eighth century B.C.

In later times Oliver La Forge tells of the use by Indians of the Pacific Northwest of a money-like object called a copper. California Indians used shell money. The Aztecs used little pieces of bronze, cut into the form of a "T," and especially designed bits of cotton cloth. Transparent quills filled with grains of gold were also used, as well as grains of cocoa and blue and scarlet parrot feathers.

The Text of The Book of Mormon

THE SON OF ALMA

The account of Alma, who was the son of Alma the first, and Chief Judge over the people of Nephi, and also the High Priest over the Church. An account of the reign of the Judges, and the wars and contentions among the people. And also an account of a war between the Nephites and the Lamanites, according to the record of Alma, the first and chief Judge.

CHAPTER 1.

1. Now it came to pass that in the first year of the reign of the judges over the people of Nephi, from this time forward, king Mosiah having gone the way of all the earth, having warred a good warfare, walking uprightly before God, leaving none to reign in his stead; nevertheless he had established laws, and they were acknowledged by the people; therefore they were obliged to abide by the laws which he had made.

2. And it came to pass that in the first year of the reign of Alma in the judgment-seat, there was a man brought before him to be judged, a man who was large, and was noted for his much strength.

3. And he had gone about among the people, preaching to them that which he termed to be the word of God, bearing down against the church; declaring unto the people that every priest and teacher ought to become popular; and they ought not to labor with their hands, but that they ought to be supported by the people.

4. And he also testified unto the people that all mankind should be saved at the last day, and that they need not fear nor tremble, but that they might lift up their heads and rejoice; for the Lord had created all men, and had also redeemed all men; and, in the end, all men should have eternal life.

5. And it came to pass that he did teach these things so much that many did believe on his words, even so many that they began to support him and give him money.

6. And he began to be lifted up in the pride of his heart, and to wear very costly apparel, yea, and even began to establish a church after the manner of his preaching.

7. And it came to pass as he was going, to preach to those who believed on his word, he met a man who belonged to the church of God, yea, even one of their teachers; and he began to contend with him sharply, that he might lead away the people of the church; but the man withstood him, admonishing him with the words of God.

8. Now the name of the man was Gideon; and it was he who was an instrument in the hands of God in delivering the people of Limhi out of bondage.

9. Now, because Gideon withstood him with the words of God he was wroth with Gideon, and drew his sword and began to smite him. Now Gideon being stricken with many years, therefore he was not able to withstand his blows, therefore he was slain by the sword.

10. And the man who slew him was taken by the people of the church, and was brought before Alma, to be judged according to the crimes which he had committed.

11. And it came to pass that he stood before Alma and pleaded for himself with much boldness.

12. But Alma said unto him: Behold, this is the first time that priestcraft has been introduced among this people. And behold, thou are not only guilty of priestcraft, but hast endeavored to enforce it by the sword; and were priestcraft to be enforced among this people it would prove their entire destruction.

13. And thou hast shed the blood of a righteous man, yea, a man who has done much good among this people; and were we to spare thee his blood would come upon us for vengeance.

14. Therefore thou art condemned to die, according to the law which has been given us by Mosiah, our last king; and it has been acknowledged by this people; therefore this people must abide by the law.

15. And it came to pass that they took him; and his name was Nehor; and they carried him upon the top of the hill Manti, and there he was caused, or rather did acknowledge, between the heavens and the earth, that what he had taught to the people was contrary to the word of God; and there he suffered an ignominious death.

16. Nevertheless, this did not put an end to the spreading of priestcraft through the land; for there were many who loved the vain things of the world, and they went forth preaching false doctrines; and this they did for the sake of riches and honor.

17. Nevertheless, they durst not lie, if it were known, for fear of the law, for liars were punished; therefore they

pretended to preach according to their belief; and now the law could have no power on any man for his belief.

18. And they durst not steal, for fear of the law, for such were punished; neither durst they rob, nor murder, for he that murdered was punished unto death.

19. But it came to pass that whosoever did not belong to the church of God began to persecute those that did belong to the church of God, and had taken upon them the name of Christ.

20. Yea, they did persecute them, and afflict them with all manner of words, and this because of their humility; because they were not proud in their own eyes, and because they did impart the word of God, one with another, without money and without price.

21. Now there was a strict law among the people of the church that there should not any man, belonging to the church, arise and persecute those that did not belong to the church, and that there should be no persecution among themselves.

22. Nevertheless, there were many among them who began to be proud, and began to contend warmly with their adversaries, even unto blows; yea, they would smite one another with their fists.

23. Now this was in the second year of the reign of Alma, and it was a cause of much affliction to the church; yea, it was the cause of much trial with the church.

24. For the hearts of many were hardened, and their names were blotted out, that they were remembered no more among the people of God. And also many withdrew themselves from among them.

25. Now this was a great trial to those that did stand fast in the faith; nevertheless, they were steadfast and immovable in keeping the commandments of God, and they bore with patience the persecution which was heaped upon them.

26. And when the priests left their labor to impart the word of God unto the people, the people also left their labors to hear the word of God. And when the priest had imparted unto them the word of God they all returned again diligently unto their labors; and the priest, not esteeming himself above his hearers, for the preacher was no better than the hearer, neither was the teacher any better than the learner; and thus they were all equal, and they did all labor, every man according to his strength.

27. And they did impart of their substance, every man according to that which he had, to the poor, and the needy, and the sick, and the afflicted; and they did not wear costly apparel, yet they were neat and comely.

28. And thus they did establish the affairs of the church; and thus they began to have continual peace again, notwithstanding all their persecutions.

29. And now, because of the steadiness of the church

they began to be exceeding rich, having abundance of all things whatsoever they stood in need—and abundance of flocks and herds, and fatlings of every kind, and also abundance of grain, and of gold, and of silver, and of precious things, and abundance of silk and fine-twined linen, and all manner of good homely cloth.

30. And thus, in their prosperous circumstances, they did not send away any who were naked, or that were hungry, or that were athirst, or that were sick, or that had not been nourished; and they did not set their hearts upon riches; therefore they were liberal to all, both old and young, both bond and free, both male and female, whether out of the church or in the church, having no respect to persons as to those who stood in need.

31. And thus they did prosper and become far more wealthy than those who did not belong to their church.

32. For those who did not belong to their church did indulge themselves in sorceries, and in idolatry or idleness, and in babblings, and in envyings and strife; wearing costly apparel; being lifted up in the pride of their own eyes; lying, thieving, robbing, committing whoredoms, and murdering, and all manner of wickedness; nevertheless, the law was put in force upon all those who did transgress it, inasmuch as it was possible.

33. And it came to pass that by thus exercising the law upon them, every man suffering according to that which he had done, they became more still, and durst not commit any wickedness if it were known; therefore, there was much peace among the people of Nephi until the fifth year of the reign of the judges.

CHAPTER 2.

1. And it came to pass in the commencement of the fifth year of their reign there began to be a contention among the people; for a certain man, being called Amlici, he being a very cunning man, yea, a wise man as to the wisdom of the world, he being after the order of the man that slew Gideon by the sword, who was executed according to the law—

2. Now this Amlici had, by his cunning, drawn away much people after him; even so much that they began to be very powerful; and they began to endeavor to establish Amlici to be king over the people.

3. Now this was alarming to the people of the church, and also to all those who had not been drawn away after the persuasions of Amlici; for they knew that according to their law that such things must be established by the voice of the people.

4. Therefore, if it were possible that Amlici should gain the voice of the people, he, being a wicked man, would deprive them of their rights and privileges of the church;

for it was his intent to destroy the church of God.

5. And it came to pass that the people assembled themselves together throughout all the land, every man according to his mind, whether it were for or against Amlici, in separate bodies, having much dispute and wonderful contentions one with another.

6. And thus they did assemble themselves together to cast in their voices concerning the matter; and they were laid before the judges.

7. And it came to pass that the voice of the people came against Amlici, that he was not made king over the people.

8. Now this did cause much joy in the hearts of those who were against him; but Amlici did stir up those who were in his favor to anger against those who were not in his favor.

9. And it came to pass that they gathered themselves together, and did consecrate Amlici to be their king.

10. Now when Amlici was made king over them he commanded them that they should take up arms against their brethren; and this he did that he might subject them to him.

11. Now the people of Amlici were distinguished by the name of Amlici, being called Amlicites; and the remainder were called Nephites, or the people of God.

12. Therefore the people of the Nephites were aware of the intent of the Amlicites, and therefore they did prepare to meet them; yea, they did arm themselves with swords, and with cimeters, and with bows, and with arrows, and with stones, and with slings, and with all manner of weapons of war, of every kind.

13. And thus they were prepared to meet the Amlicites at the time of their coming. And there were appointed captains, and higher captains, and chief captains, according to their numbers.

14. And it came to pass that Amlici did arm his men with all manner of weapons of war of every kind; and he also appointed rulers and leaders over his people, to lead them to war against their brethren.

15. And it came to pass that the Amlicites came upon the hill Amnihu, which was east of the river Sidon, which ran by the land of Zarahemla, and there they began to make war with the Nephites.

16. Now Alma, being the chief judge and the governor of the people of Nephi, therefore he went up with his people, yea, with his captains, and chief captains, yea, at the head of his armies, against the Amlicites to battle.

17. And they began to slay the Amlicites upon the hill east of Sidon. And the Amlicites did contend with the Nephites with great strength, insomuch that many of the Nephites did fall before the Amlicites.

18. Nevertheless the Lord did strengthen the hand of the Nephites, that they slew the Amlicites with great slaughter, that they began to flee before them.

19. And it came to pass that the Nephites did pursue the Amlicites all that day, and did slay them with much slaughter, insomuch that there were slain of the Amlicites twelve thousand five hundred thirty and two souls; and there were slain of the Nephites six thousand five hundred sixty and two souls.

20. And it came to pass that when Alma could pursue the Amlicites no longer he caused that his people should pitch their tents in the valley of Gideon, the valley being called after that Gideon who was slain by the hand of Nehor with the sword; and in this valley the Nephites did pitch their tents for the night.

21. And Alma sent spies to follow the remnant of the Amlicites, that he might know of their plans and their plots, whereby he might guard himself against them, that he might preserve his people from being destroyed.

22. Now those whom he had sent out to watch the camp of the Amlicites were called Zeram, and Amnor, and Manti, and Limher; these were they who went out with their men to watch the camp of the Amlicites.

23. And it came to pass that on the morrow they returned into the camp of the Nephites in great haste, being greatly astonished, and struck with much fear, saying:

24. Behold, we followed the camp of the Amlicites, and to our great astonishment, in the land of Minon, above the land of Zarahemla, in the course of the land of Nephi, we saw a numerous host of the Lamanites; and behold, the Amlicites have joined them;

25. And they are upon our brethren in that land; and they are fleeing before them with their flocks, and their wives, and their children, towards our city; and except we make haste they obtain possession of our city, and our fathers, and our wives, and our children be slain.

26. And it came to pass that the people of Nephi took their tents, and departed out of the valley of Gideon towards their city, which was the city of Zarahemla.

27. And behold, as they were crossing the river Sidon, the Lamanites and the Amlicites, being as numerous almost, as it were, as the sands of the sea, came upon them to destroy them.

28. Nevertheless, the Nephites being strengthened by the hand of the Lord, having prayed mightily to him that he would deliver them out of the hands of their enemies, therefore the Lord did hear their cries, and did strengthen them, and the Lamanites and the Amlicites did fall before them.

29. And it came to pass that Alma fought with Amlici with the sword, face to face; and they did contend mightily, one with another.

30. And it came to pass that Alma, being a man of

God, being exercised with much faith, cried, saying: O Lord, have mercy and spare my life, that I may be an instrument in thy hands to save and preserve this people.

31. Now when Alma had said these words he contended again with Amlici; and he was strengthened, insomuch that he slew Amlici with the sword.

32. And he also contended with the king of the Lamanites; but the king of the Lamanites fled back from before Alma and sent his guards to contend with Alma.

33. But Alma, with his guards, contended with the guards of the king of the Lamanites until he slew and drove them back.

34. And thus he cleared the ground, or rather the bank, which was on the west of the river Sidon, throwing the bodies of the Lamanites who had been slain into the waters of Sidon, that thereby his people might have room to cross and contend with the Lamanites and the Amlicites on the west side of the river Sidon.

35. And it came to pass that when they had all crossed the river Sidon that the Lamanites and the Amlicites began to flee before them, notwithstanding they were so numerous that they could not be numbered.

36. And they fled before the Nephites towards the wilderness which was west and north, away beyond the borders of the land; and the Nephites did pursue them with their might, and did slay them.

37. Yea, they were met on every hand, and slain and driven, until they were scattered on the west, and on the north, until they had reached the wilderness, which was called Hermounts; and it was that part of the wilderness which was infested by wild and ravenous beasts.

38. And it came to pass that many died in the wilderness of their wounds, and were devoured by those beasts and also the vultures of the air; and their bones have been found, and have been heaped up on the earth.

CHAPTER 3.

1. And it came to pass that the Nephites who were not slain by the weapons of war, after having buried those who had been slain—now the number of the slain were not numbered, because of the greatness of their number—after they had finished burying their dead they all returned to their lands, and to their houses, and their wives, and their children.

2. Now many women and children had been slain with the sword, and also many of their flocks and their herds; and also many of their fields of grain were destroyed, for they were trodden down by the hosts of men.

3. And now as many of the Lamanites and the Amlicites who had been slain upon the bank of the river Sidon were cast into the waters of Sidon; and behold their bones are in the depths of the sea, and they are many.

4. And the Amlicites were distinguished from the Nephites, for they had marked themselves with red in their foreheads after the manner of the Lamanites; nevertheless they had not shorn their heads like unto the Lamanites.

5. Now the heads of the Lamanites were shorn; and they were naked, save it were skin which was girded about their loins, and also their armor, which was girded about them, and their bows, and their arrows, and their stones, and their slings, and so forth.

6. And the skins of the Lamanites were dark, according to the mark which was set upon their fathers, which was a curse upon them because of their transgression and their rebellion against their brethren, who consisted of Nephi, Jacob, and Joseph, and Sam, who were just and holy men.

7. And their brethren sought to destroy them, therefore they were cursed; and the Lord God set a mark upon them, yea, upon Laman and Lemuel, and also the sons of Ishmael, and Ishmaelitish women.

8. And this was done that their seed might be distinguished from the seed of their brethren, that thereby the Lord God might preserve his people, that they might not mix and believe in incorrect traditions which would prove their destruction.

9. And it came to pass that whosoever did mingle his seed with that of the Lamanites did bring the same curse upon his seed.

10. Therefore, whosoever suffered himself to be led away by the Lamanites was called under that head, and there was a mark set upon him.

11. And it came to pass that whosoever would not believe in the tradition of the Lamanites, but believed those records which were brought out of the land of Jerusalem, and also in the tradition of their fathers, which were correct, who believed in the commandments of God and kept them, were called the Nephites, or the people of Nephi, from that time forth—

12. And it is they who have kept the records which are true of their people, and also of the people of the Lamanites.

13. Now we will return again to the Amlicites, for they also had a mark set upon them; yea, they set the mark upon themselves, yea, even a mark of red upon their foreheads.

14. Thus the word of God is fulfilled, for these are the words which he said to Nephi: Behold, the Lamanites have I cursed, and I will set a mark on them that they and

their seed may be separated from thee and thy seed, from this time henceforth and forever, except they repent of their wickedness and turn to me that I may have mercy upon them.

15. And again: I will set a mark upon him that mingleth his seed with thy brethren, that they may be cursed also.

16. And again: I will set a mark upon him that fighteth against thee and thy seed.

17. And again, I say he that departeth from thee shall no more be called thy seed; and I will bless thee, and whomsoever shall be called thy seed, henceforth and forever; and these were the promises of the Lord unto Nephi and to his seed.

18. Now the Amlicites knew not that they were fulfilling the words of God when they began to mark themselves in their foreheads; nevertheless they had come out in open rebellion against God; therefore it was expedient that the curse should fall upon them.

19. Now I would that ye should see that they brought upon themselves the curse; and even so doth every man that is cursed bring upon himself his own condemnation.

20. Now it came to pass that not many days after the battle which was fought in the land of Zarahemla, by the Lamanites and the Amlicites, that there was another army of the Lamanites came in upon the people of Nephi, in the same place where the first army met the Amlicites.

21. And it came to pass that there was an army sent to drive them out of their land.

22. Now Alma himself being afflicted with a wound did not go up to battle at this time against the Lamanites;

23. But he sent up a numerous army against them; and they went up and slew many of the Lamanites, and drove the remainder of them out of the borders of their land.

24. And then they returned again and began to establish peace in the land, being troubled no more for a time with their enemies.

25. Now all these things were done, yea, all these wars and contentions were commenced and ended in the fifth year of the reign of the judges.

26. And in one year were thousands and tens of thousands of souls sent to the eternal world, that they might reap their rewards according to their works, whether they were good or whether they were bad, to reap eternal happiness or eternal misery, according to the spirit which they listed to obey, whether it be a good spirit or a bad one.

27. For every man receiveth wages of him whom he listeth to obey, and this according to the words of the spirit of prophecy; therefore let it be according to the truth. And thus endeth the fifth year of the reign of the judges.

CHAPTER 4.

1. Now it came to pass in the sixth year of the reign of the judges over the people of Nephi, there were no contentions nor wars in the land of Zarahemla;

2. But the people were afflicted, yea, greatly afflicted for the loss of their brethren, and also for the loss of their flocks and herds, and also for the loss of their fields of grain, which were trodden under foot and destroyed by the Lamanites.

3. And so great were their afflictions that every soul had cause to mourn; and they believed that it was the judgments of God sent upon them because of their wickedness and their abominations; therefore they were awakened to a remembrance of their duty.

4. And they began to establish the church more fully; yea, and many were baptized in the waters of Sidon and were joined to the church of God; yea, they were baptized by the hand of Alma, who had been consecrated the high priest over the people of the church, by the hand of his father Alma.

5. And it came to pass in the seventh year of the reign of the judges there were about three thousand five hundred souls that united themselves to the church of God and were baptized. And thus endeth the seventh year of the reign of the judges over the people of Nephi; and there was continual peace in all that time.

6. And it came to pass in the eighth year of the reign of the judges, that the people of the church began to wax proud, because of their exceeding riches, and their fine silks, and their fine-twined linen, and because of their many flocks and herds, and their gold and their silver, and all manner of precious things, which they had obtained by their industry; and in all these things were they lifted up in the pride of their eyes, for they began to wear very costly apparel.

7. Now this was the cause of much affliction to Alma, yea, and to many of the people whom Alma had consecrated to be teachers, and priests, and elders over the church; yea, many of them were sorely grieved for the wickedness which they saw had begun to be among their people.

8. For they saw and beheld with great sorrow that the people of the church began to be lifted up in the pride of their eyes, and to set their hearts upon riches and upon the vain things of the world, that they began to be scornful, one towards another, and they began to persecute those that did not believe according to their own will and pleasure.

9. And thus, in this eighth year of the reign of the judges, there began to be great contentions among the

people of the church; yea, there were envyings, and strife, and malice, and persecutions, and pride, even to exceed the pride of those who did not belong to the church of God.

10. And thus ended the eighth year of the reign of the judges; and the wickedness of the church was a great stumbling-block to those who did not belong to the church; and thus the church began to fail in its progress.

11. And it came to pass in the commencement of the ninth year, Alma saw the wickedness of the church, and he saw also that the example of the church began to lead those who were unbelievers on from one piece of iniquity to another, thus bringing on the destruction of the people.

12. Yea, he saw great inequality among the people, some lifting themselves up with their pride, despising others, turning their backs upon the needy and the naked and those who were hungry, and those who were athirst, and those who were sick and afflicted.

13. Now this was a great cause for lamentations among the people, while others were abasing themselves, succoring those who stood in need of their succor, such as imparting their substance to the poor and the needy, feeding the hungry, and suffering all manner of afflictions, for Christ's sake, who should come according to the spirit of prophecy;

14. Looking forward to that day, thus retaining a remission of their sins; being filled with great joy because of the resurrection of the dead, according to the will and power and deliverance of Jesus Christ from the bands of death.

15. And now it came to pass that Alma, having seen the afflictions of the humble followers of God, and the persecutions which were heaped upon them by the remainder of his people, and seeing all their inequality, began to be very sorrowful; nevertheless the Spirit of the Lord did not fail him.

16. And he selected a wise man who was among the elders of the church, and gave him power according to the voice of the people, that he might have power to enact laws according to the laws which had been given, and to put them in force according to the wickedness and the crimes of the people.

17. Now this man's name was Nephihah, and he was appointed chief judge; and he sat in the judgment-seat to judge and to govern the people.

18. Now Alma did not grant unto him the office of being high priest over the church, but he retained the office of high priest unto himself; but he delivered the judgment-seat unto Nephihah.

19. And this he did that he himself might go forth among his people, or among the people of Nephi, that he might preach the word of God unto them, to stir them up in remembrance of their duty, and that he might pull down, by the word of God, all the pride and craftiness and all the contentions which were among his people, seeing no way that he might reclaim them save it were in bearing down in pure testimony against them.

20. And thus in the commencement of the ninth year of the reign of the judges over the people of Nephi, Alma delivered up the judgment-seat to Nephihah, and confined himself wholly to the high priesthood of the holy order of God, to the testimony of the word, according to the spirit of revelation and prophecy.

CHAPTER 5.

The words which Alma, the High Priest according to the holy order of God, delivered to the people in their cities and villages throughout the land.

1. Now it came to pass that Alma began to deliver the word of God unto the people, first in the land of Zarahemla, and from thence throughout all the land.

2. And these are the words which he spake to the people in the church which was established in the city of Zarahemla, according to his own record, saying:

3. I, Alma, having been consecrated by my father, Alma, to be a high priest over the church of God, he having power and authority from God to do these things, behold, I say unto you that he began to establish a church in the land which was in the borders of Nephi; yea, the land which was called the land of Mormon; yea, and he did baptize his brethren in the waters of Mormon.

4. And behold, I say unto you, they were delivered out of the hands of the people of king Noah, by the mercy and power of God.

5. And behold, after that, they were brought into bondage by the hands of the Lamanites in the wilderness; yea, I say unto you, they were in captivity, and again the Lord did deliver them out of bondage by the power of his word; and we were brought into this land, and here we began to establish the church of God throughout this land also.

6. And now behold, I say unto you, my brethren, you that belong to this church, have you sufficiently retained in remembrance the captivity of your fathers? Yea, and have you sufficiently retained in remembrance his mercy and long-suffering towards them? And moreover, have ye sufficiently retained in remembrance that he has delivered their souls from hell?

7. Behold, he changed their hearts; yea, he awakened them out of a deep sleep, and they awoke unto God. Behold, they were in the midst of darkness; nevertheless, their souls were illuminated by the light of the everlasting

word; yea, they were encircled about by the bands of death, and the chains of hell, and an everlasting destruction did await them.

8. And now I ask of you, my brethren, were they destroyed? Behold, I say unto you, Nay, they were not.

9. And again I ask, were the bands of death broken, and the chains of hell which encircled them about, were they loosed? I say unto you, Yea, they were loosed, and their souls did expand, and they did sing redeeming love. And I say unto you that they are saved.

10. And now I ask of you on what conditions are they saved? Yea, what grounds had they to hope for salvation? What is the cause of their being loosed from the bands of death, yea, and also the chains of hell?

11. Behold, I can tell you—did not my father Alma believe in the words which were delivered by the mouth of Abinadi? And was he not a holy prophet? Did he not speak the words of God, and my father Alma believe them?

12. And according to his faith there was a mighty change wrought in his heart. Behold I say unto you that this is all true.

13. And behold, he preached the word unto your fathers, and a mighty change was also wrought in their hearts, and they humbled themselves and put their trust in the true and living God. And behold, they were faithful until the end; therefore they were saved.

14. And now behold, I ask of you, my brethren of the church, have ye spiritually been born of God? Have ye received his image in your countenances? Have ye experienced this mighty change in your hearts?

15. Do ye exercise faith in the redemption of him who created you? Do you look forward with an eye of faith, and view this mortal body raised in immortality, and this corruption raised in incorruption, to stand before God to be judged according to the deeds which have been done in the mortal body?

16. I say unto you, can you imagine to yourselves that ye hear the voice of the Lord, saying unto you, in that day: Come unto me ye blessed, for behold, your works have been the works of righteousness upon the face of the earth?

17. Or do ye imagine to yourselves that ye can lie unto the Lord in that day, and say—Lord, our works have been righteous works upon the face of the earth—and that he will save you?

18. Or otherwise, can ye imagine yourselves brought before the tribunal of God with your souls filled with guilt and remorse, having a remembrance of all your guilt, yea, a perfect remembrance of all your wickedness, yea, a remembrance that ye have set at defiance the commandments of God?

19. I say unto you, can ye look up to God at that day with a pure heart and clean hands? I say unto you, can you look up, having the image of God engraven upon your countenances?

20. I say unto you, can ye think of being saved when you have yielded yourselves to become subjects to the devil?

21. I say unto you, ye will know at that day that ye cannot be saved; for there can no man be saved except his garments are washed white; yea, his garments must be purified until they are cleansed from all stain, through the blood of him of whom it has been spoken by our fathers, who should come to redeem his people from their sins.

22. And now I ask of you, my brethren, how will any of you feel, if ye shall stand before the bar of God, having your garments stained with blood and all manner of filthiness? Behold, what will these things testify against you?

23. Behold will they not testify that ye are murderers, yea, and also that ye are guilty of all manner of wickedness?

24. Behold, my brethren, do ye suppose that such an one can have a place to sit down in the kingdom of God, with Abraham, with Isaac, and with Jacob, and also all the holy prophets, whose garments are cleansed and are spotless, pure and white?

25. I say unto you, Nay; except ye make our Creator a liar from the beginning, or suppose that he is a liar from the beginning, ye cannot suppose that such can have place in the kingdom of heaven; but they shall be cast out for they are the children of the kingdom of the devil.

26. And now behold, I say unto you, my brethren, if ye have experienced a change of heart, and if ye have felt to sing the song of redeeming love, I would ask, can ye feel so now?

27. Have ye walked, keeping yourselves blameless before God? Could ye say, if ye were called to die at this time, within yourselves, that ye have been sufficiently humble? That your garments have been cleansed and made white through the blood of Christ, who will come to redeem his people from their sins?

28. Behold, are ye stripped of pride? I say unto you, if ye are not ye are not prepared to meet God. Behold ye must prepare quickly; for the kingdom of heaven is soon at hand, and such an one hath not eternal life.

29. Behold, I say, is there one among you who is not stripped of envy? I say unto you that such an one is not prepared; and I would that he should prepare quickly, for the hour is close at hand, and he knoweth not when the time shall come; for such an one is not found guiltless.

30. And again I say unto you, is there one among you that doth make a mock of his brother, or that heapeth upon him persecutions?

31. Wo unto such an one, for he is not prepared, and the time is at hand that he must repent or he cannot be saved!

32.   Yea, even wo unto all ye workers of iniquity; repent, repent, for the Lord God hath spoken it!

33.   Behold, he sendeth an invitation unto all men, for the arms of mercy are extended towards them, and he saith: Repent, and I will receive you.

34.   Yea, he saith: Come unto me and ye shall partake of the fruit of the tree of life; yea, ye shall eat and drink of the bread and the waters of life freely;

35.   Yea, come unto me and bring forth works of righteousness, and ye shall not be hewn down and cast into the fire—

36.   For behold, the time is at hand that whosoever bringeth forth not good fruit, or whosoever doeth not the works of righteousness, the same have cause to wail and mourn.

37.   O ye workers of iniquity; ye that are puffed up in the vain things of the world, ye that have professed to have known the ways of righteousness nevertheless have gone astray, as sheep having no shepherd, notwithstanding a shepherd hath called after you and is still calling after you, but ye will not hearken unto his voice!

38.   Behold, I say unto you, that the good shepherd doth call you; yea, and in his own name he doth call you, which is the name of Christ; and if ye will not hearken unto the voice of the good shepherd, to the name by which ye are called, behold, ye are not the sheep of the good shepherd.

39.   And now if ye are not the sheep of the good shepherd, of what fold are ye? Behold, I say unto you, that the devil is your shepherd, and ye are of his fold; and now, who can deny this? Behold, I say unto you, whosoever denieth this is a liar and a child of the devil.

40.   For I say unto you that whatsoever is good cometh from God, and whatsoever is evil cometh from the devil.

41.   Therefore, if a man bringeth forth good works he hearkeneth unto the voice of the good shepherd, and he doth follow him; but whosoever bringeth forth evil works, the same becometh a child of the devil, for he hearkeneth unto his voice, and doth follow him.

42.   And whosoever doeth this must receive his wages of him; therefore, for his wages he receiveth death, as to things pertaining unto righteousness, being dead unto all good works.

43.   And now, my brethren, I would that ye should hear me, for I speak in the energy of my soul; for behold, I have spoken unto you plainly that ye cannot err, or have spoken according to the commandments of God.

44.   For I am called to speak after this manner, according to the holy order of God, which is in Christ Jesus; yea, I am commanded to stand and testify unto this people the things which have been spoken by our fathers con-cerning the things which are to come.

45.   And this is not all. Do ye not suppose that I know of these things myself? Behold, I testify unto you that I do know that these things whereof I have spoken are true. And how do ye suppose that I know of their surety?

46.   Behold, I say unto you they are made known unto me by the Holy Spirit of God. Behold, I have fasted and prayed many days that I might know these things of myself. And now I do know of myself that they are true; for the Lord God hath made them manifest unto me by his Holy Spirit; and this is the spirit of revelation which is in me.

47.   And moreover, I say unto you that it has thus been revealed unto me, that the words which have been spoken by our fathers are true, even so according to the spirit of prophecy which is in me, which is also by the manifestation of the Spirit of God.

48.   I say unto you, that I know of myself that whatsoever I shall say unto you, concerning that which is to come, is true; and I say unto you, that I know that Jesus Christ shall come, yea, the Son, the Only Begotten of the Father, full of grace, and mercy, and truth. And behold, it is he that cometh to take away the sins of the world, yea, the sins of every man who steadfastly believeth on his name.

49.   And now I say unto you that this is the order after which I am called, yea, to preach unto my beloved brethren, yea, and every one that dwelleth in the land; yea, to preach unto all, both old and young, both bond and free; yea, I say unto you the aged, and also the middle aged, and the rising generation; yea, to cry unto them that they must repent and be born again.

50.   Yea, thus saith the Spirit: Repent, all ye ends of the earth, for the kingdom of heaven is soon at hand; yea, the Son of God cometh in his glory, in his might, majesty, power, and dominion. Yea, my beloved brethren, I say unto you, that the Spirit saith: Behold the glory of the King of all the earth; and also the King of heaven shall very soon shine forth among all the children of men.

51.   And also the Spirit saith unto me, yea, crieth unto me with a mighty voice, saying: Go forth and say unto this people—Repent, for except ye repent ye can in nowise inherit the kingdom of heaven.

52.   And again I say unto you, the Spirit saith: Behold, the ax is laid at the root of the tree; therefore every tree that bringeth not forth good fruit shall be hewn down and cast into the fire, yea, a fire which cannot be consumed, even an unquenchable fire. Behold, and remember, the Holy One hath spoken it.

53.   And now my beloved brethren, I say unto you,

can ye withstand these sayings; yea, can ye lay aside these things, and trample the Holy One under your feet; yea, can ye be puffed up in the pride of your hearts; yea, will ye still persist in the wearing of costly apparel and setting your hearts upon the vain things of the world, upon your riches?

54. Yea, will ye persist in supposing that ye are better one than another; yea, will ye persist in the persecution of your brethren, who humble themselves and do walk after the holy order of God, wherewith they have been brought into this church, having been sanctified by the Holy Spirit, and they do bring forth works which are meet for repentance—

55. Yea, and will you persist in turning your backs upon the poor, and the needy, and in withholding your substance from them?

56. And finally, all ye that will persist in your wickedness, I say unto you that these are they who shall be hewn down and cast into the fire except they speedily repent.

57. And now I say unto you, all you that are desirous to follow the voice of the good shepherd, come ye out from the wicked, and be ye separate, and touch not their unclean things; and behold, their names shall be blotted out, that the names of the wicked shall not be numbered among the names of the righteous, that the word of God may be fulfilled, which saith: The names of the wicked shall not be mingled with the names of my people;

58. For the names of the righteous shall be written in the book of life, and unto them will I grant an inheritance at my right hand. And now, my brethren, what have ye to say against this? I say unto you, if ye speak against it, it matters not, for the word of God must be fulfilled.

59. For what shepherd is there among you having many sheep doth not watch over them, that the wolves enter not and devour his flock? And behold, if a wolf enter his flock doth he not drive him out? Yea, and at the last, if he can, he will destroy him.

60. And now I say unto you that the good shepherd doth call after you; and if you will hearken unto his voice he will bring you into his fold, and ye are his sheep; and he commandeth you that ye suffer no ravenous wolf to enter among you, that ye may not be destroyed.

61. And now I, Alma, do command you in the language of him who hath commanded me, that ye observe to do the words which I have spoken unto you.

62. I speak by way of command unto you that belong to the church; and unto those who do not belong to the church I speak by way of invitation, saying: Come and be baptized unto repentance, that ye also may be partakers of the fruit of the tree of life.

CHAPTER 6.

1. And now it came to pass that after Alma had made an end of speaking unto the people of the church, which was established in the city of Zarahemla, he ordained priests and elders, by laying on his hands according to the order of God, to preside and watch over the church.

2. And it came to pass that whosoever did not belong to the church who repented of their sins were baptized unto repentance, and were received into the church.

3. And it also came to pass that whosoever did belong to the church that did not repent of their wickedness and humble themselves before God—I mean those who were lifted up in the pride of their hearts—the same were rejected, and their names were blotted out, that their names were not numbered among those of the righteous.

4. And thus they began to establish the order of the church in the city of Zarahemla.

5. Now I would that ye should understand that the word of God was liberal unto all, that none were deprived of the privilege of assembling themselves together to hear the word of God.

6. Nevertheless the children of God were commanded that they should gather themselves together oft, and join in fasting and mighty prayer in behalf of the welfare of the souls of those who knew not God.

7. And now it came to pass that when Alma had made these regulations he departed from them, yea, from the church which was in the city of Zarahemla, and went over upon the east of the river Sidon, into the valley of Gideon, there having been a city built, which was called the city of Gideon, which was in the valley that was called Gideon, being called after the man who was slain by the hand of Nehor with the sword.

8. And Alma went and began to declare the word of God unto the church which was established in the valley of Gideon, according to the revelation of the truth of the word which had been spoken by his fathers, and according to the spirit of prophecy which was in him, according to the testimony of Jesus Christ, the Son of God, who should come to redeem his people from their sins, and the holy order by which he was called. And thus it is written. Amen.

CHAPTER 7.

1. Behold my beloved brethren, seeing that I have been permitted to come unto you, therefore I attempt to address you in my language; yea, by my own mouth, seeing that it is the first time that I have spoken unto you

by the words of my mouth, I having been wholly confined to the judgment-seat, having had much business that I could not come unto you.

2. And even I could not have come now at this time were it not that the judgment-seat hath been given to another, to reign in my stead; and the Lord in much mercy hath granted that I should come unto you.

3. And behold, I have come having great hopes and much desire that I should find that ye had humbled yourselves before God, and that ye had continued in the supplicating of his grace, that I should find that ye were blameless before him, that I should find that ye were not in the awful dilemma that our brethren were in at Zarahemla.

4. And blessed be the name of God, that he hath given me to know, yea, hath given unto me the exceeding great joy of knowing that they are established again in the way of his righteousness.

5. And I trust, according to the Spirit of God which is in me, that I shall also have joy over you; nevertheless I do not desire that my joy over you should come by the cause of so much afflictions and sorrow which I have had for the brethren at Zarahemla, for behold, my joy cometh over them after wading through much affliction and sorrow.

6. And behold, I trust that ye are not in a state of so much unbelief as were your brethren; I trust that ye are not lifted up in the pride of your hearts; yea, I trust that ye have not set your hearts upon riches and the vain things of the world; yea, I trust that you do not worship idols, but that ye do worship the true and living God, and that ye look forward for the remission of your sins, with an everlasting faith, which is to come.

7. For behold, I say unto you there be many things to come; and behold, there is one thing which is of more importance than they all—for behold, the time is not far distant that the Redeemer liveth and cometh among his people.

8. Behold, I do not say that he will come among us at the time of his dwelling in his mortal tabernacle; for behold, the Spirit hath not said unto me that this should be the case. Now as to this thing I do not know; but this much I do know, that the Lord God hath power to do all things which are according to his word.

9. But behold, the Spirit hath said this much unto me, saying: Cry unto this people, saying—Repent ye, and prepare the way of the Lord, and walk in his paths, which are straight; for behold, the kingdom of heaven is at hand, and the Son of God cometh upon the face of the earth.

10. And behold, he shall be born of Mary, at Jerusalem which is the land of our forefathers, she being a virgin, a precious and chosen vessel, who shall be overshadowed and conceive by the power of the Holy Ghost, and bring forth a son, yea, even the Son of God.

11. And he shall go forth, suffering pains and afflictions and temptations of every kind; and this that the word might be fulfilled which saith he will take upon him the pains and the sicknesses of his people.

12. And he will take upon him death, that he may loose the bands of death which bind his people; and he will take upon him their infirmities, that his bowels may be filled with mercy, according to the flesh, that he may know according to the flesh how to succor his people according to their infirmities.

13. Now the Spirit knoweth all things; nevertheless the Son of God suffereth according to the flesh that he might take upon him the sins of his people, that he might blot out their transgressions according to the power of his deliverance; and now behold, this is the testimony which is in me.

14. Now I say unto you that ye must repent, and be born again; for the Spirit saith if ye are not born again ye cannot inherit the kingdom of heaven; therefore come and be baptized unto repentance, that ye may be washed from your sins, that ye may have faith on the Lamb of God, who taketh away the sins of the world, who is mighty to save and to cleanse from all unrighteousness.

15. Yea, I say unto you come and fear not, and lay aside every sin, which easily doth beset you, which doth bind you down to destruction, yea, come and go forth, and show unto your God that ye are willing to repent of your sins and enter into a covenant with him to keep his commandments, and witness it unto him this day by going into the waters of baptism.

16. And whosoever doeth this, and keepeth the commandments of God from thenceforth, the same will remember that I say unto him, yea, he will remember that I have said unto him, he shall have eternal life, according to the testimony of the Holy Spirit, which testifieth in me.

17. And now my beloved brethren, do you believe these things? Behold, I say unto you, yea, I know that ye believe them; and the way that I know that ye believe them is by the manifestation of the Spirit which is in me. And now because your faith is strong concerning that, yea, concerning the things which I have spoken, great is my joy.

18. For as I said unto you from the beginning, that I had much desire that ye were not in the state of dilemma like your brethren, even so I have found that my desires have been gratified.

19. For I perceive that ye are in the paths of righteousness; I perceive that ye are in the path which leads to the kingdom of God; yea, I perceive that ye are making his paths straight.

20. I perceive that it has been made known unto you, by the testimony of his word, that he cannot walk in crooked paths; neither doth he vary from that which

he hath said; neither hath he a shadow of turning from the right to the left, or from that which is right to that which is wrong; therefore, his course is one eternal round.

21. And he doth not dwell in unholy temples; neither can filthiness or anything which is unclean be received into the kingdom of God; therefore I say unto you the time shall come, yea, and it shall be at the last day, that he who is filthy shall remain in his filthiness.

22. And now my beloved brethren, I have said these things unto you that I might awaken you to a sense of your duty to God, that ye may walk blameless before him, that ye may walk after the holy order of God, after which ye have been received.

23. And now I would that ye should be humble, and be submissive and gentle; easy to be entreated; full of patience and long-suffering; being temperate in all things; being diligent in keeping the commandments of God at all times; asking for whatsoever things ye stand in need, both spiritual and temporal; always returning thanks unto God for whatsoever things ye do receive.

24. And see that ye have faith, hope, and charity, and then ye will always abound in good works.

25. And may the Lord bless you, and keep your garments spotless, that ye may at last be brought to sit down with Abraham, Isaac, and Jacob, and the holy prophets who have been ever since the world began, having your garments spotless even as their garments are spotless, in the kingdom of heaven to go no more out.

26. And now my beloved brethren, I have spoken these words unto you according to the Spirit which testifieth in me; and my soul doth exceedingly rejoice, because of the exceeding diligence and heed which ye have given unto my word.

27. And now, may the peace of God rest upon you, and upon your houses and lands, and upon your flocks and herds, and all that you possess, your women and your children, according to your faith and good works, from this time forth and forever. And thus I have spoken. Amen.

CHAPTER 8.

1. And now it came to pass that Alma returned from the land of Gideon, after having taught the people of Gideon many things which cannot be written, having established the order of the church, according as he had before done in the land of Zarahemla, yea, he returned to his own house at Zarahemla to rest himself from the labors which he had performed.

2. And thus ended the ninth year of the reign of the judges over the people of Nephi.

3. And it came to pass in the commencement of the tenth year of the reign of the judges over the people of Nephi, that Alma departed from thence and took his journey over into the land of Melek, on the west of the river Sidon, on the west by the borders of the wilderness.

4. And he began to teach the people in the land of Melek according to the holy order of God, by which he had been called; and he began to teach the people throughout all the land of Melek.

5. And it came to pass that the people came to him throughout all the borders of the land which was by the wilderness side. And they were baptized throughout all the land;

6. So that when he had finished his work at Melek he departed thence, and traveled three days' journey on the north of the land of Melek; and he came to a city which was called Ammonihah.

7. Now it was the custom of the people of Nephi to call their lands, and their cities, and their villages, yea, even all their small villages, after the name of him who first possessed them; and thus it was with the land of Ammonihah.

8. And it came to pass that when Alma had come to the city of Ammonihah he began to preach the word of God unto them.

9. Now Satan had gotten great hold upon the hearts of the people of the city of Ammonihah; therefore they would not hearken unto the words of Alma.

10. Nevertheless Alma labored much in the spirit, wrestling with God in mighty prayer, that he would pour out his Spirit upon the people who were in the city; that he would also grant that he might baptize them unto repentance.

11. Nevertheless, they hardened their hearts, saying unto him: Behold, we know that thou art Alma; and we know that thou art high priest over the church which thou hast established in many parts of the land, according to your tradition; and we are not of thy church, and we do not believe in such foolish traditions.

12. And now we know that because we are not of thy church we know that thou hast no power over us; and thou hast delivered up the judgment-seat unto Nephihah; therefore thou art not the chief judge over us.

13. Now when the people had said this, and withstood all his words, and reviled him, and spit upon him, and caused that he should be cast out of their city, he departed thence and took his journey towards the city which was called Aaron.

14. And it came to pass that while he was journeying thither, being weighed down with sorrow, wading through much tribulation and anguish of soul, because of the wickedness of the people who were in the city of Ammonihah, it came to pass while Alma was thus weighed down with sorrow, behold an angel of the Lord appeared

unto him, saying:

15. Blessed art thou, Alma; therefore, lift up thy head and rejoice, for thou hast great cause to rejoice; for thou hast been faithful in keeping the commandments of God from the time which thou receivedst thy first message from him. Behold, I am he that delivered it unto you.

16. And behold, I am sent to command thee that thou return to the city of Ammonihah, and preach again unto the people of the city; yea, preach unto them. Yea, say unto them, except they repent the Lord God will destroy them.

17. For behold, they do study at this time that they may destroy the liberty of thy people, (for thus saith the Lord) which is contrary to the statutes, and judgments, and commandments which he has given unto his people.

18. Now it came to pass that after Alma had received his message from the angel of the Lord he returned speedily to the land of Ammonihah. And he entered the city by another way, yea, by the way which is on the south of the city of Ammonihah.

19. And as he entered the city he was an hungered, and he said to a man: Will ye give to an humble servant of God something to eat?

20. And the man said unto him: I am a Nephite, and I know that thou art a holy prophet of God, for thou art the man whom an angel said in a vision: Thou shalt receive. Therefore, go with me into my house and I will impart unto thee of my food; and I know that thou wilt be a blessing unto me and my house.

21. And it came to pass that the man received him into his house; and the man was called Amulek; and he brought forth bread and meat and set before Alma.

22. And it came to pass that Alma ate bread and was filled; and he blessed Amulek and his house, and he gave thanks unto God.

23. And after he had eaten and was filled he said unto Amulek: I am Alma, and am the high priest over the church of God throughout the land.

24. And behold, I have been called to preach the word of God among all this people, according to the spirit of revelation and prophecy; and I was in this land and they would not receive me, but they cast me out and I was about to set my back towards this land forever.

25. But behold, I have been commanded that I should turn again and prophesy unto this people, yea, and to testify against them concerning their iniquities.

26. And now, Amulek, because thou hast fed me and taken me in, thou art blessed; for I was an hungered, for I had fasted many days.

27. And Alma tarried many days with Amulek before he began to preach unto the people.

28. And it came to pass that the people did wax more gross in their iniquities.

29. And the word came to Alma, saying: Go; and also say unto my servant Amulek, go forth and prophesy unto this people, saying—Repent ye, for thus saith the Lord, except ye repent I will visit this people in mine anger; yea, and I will not turn my fierce anger away.

30. And Alma went forth, and also Amulek, among the people, to declare the words of God unto them; and they were filled with the Holy Ghost.

31. And they had power given unto them, insomuch that they could not be confined in dungeons; neither was it possible that any man could slay them; nevertheless they did not exercise their power until they were bound in bands and cast into prison. Now, this was done that the Lord might show forth his power in them.

32. And it came to pass that they went forth and began to preach and to prophesy unto the people, according to the spirit and power which the Lord had given them.

CHAPTER 9.

The words of Alma, and also the words of Amulek, which were declared unto the people who were in the land of Ammonihah. And also they are cast into prison, and delivered by the miraculous power of God which was in them, according to the record of Alma.

1. And again, I, Alma, having been commanded of God that I should take Amulek and go forth and preach again unto this people, or the people who were in the city of Ammonihah, it came to pass as I began to preach unto them, they began to contend with me, saying:

2. Who art thou? Suppose ye that we shall believe the testimony of one man, although he should preach unto us that the earth should pass away?

3. Now they understood not the words which they spake; for they knew not that the earth should pass away.

4. And they said also: We will not believe thy words if thou shouldst prophesy that this great city should be destroyed in one day.

5. Now they knew not that God could do such marvelous works, for they were a hard-hearted and a stiffnecked people.

6. And they said: Who is God, that sendeth no more authority than one man among his people, to declare unto them the truth of such great and marvelous things?

7. And they stood forth to lay their hands on me; but behold, they did not. And I stood with boldness to declare unto them, yea, I did boldly testify unto them saying:

8. Behold, O ye wicked and perverse generation, how have ye forgotten the tradition of your fathers; yea, how soon ye have forgotten the commandments of God.

9. Do ye not remember that our father, Lehi, was brought out of Jerusalem by the hand of God? Do ye not remember that they were all led by him through the wilderness?

10. And have ye forgotten so soon how many times he delivered our fathers out of the hands of their enemies, and preserved them from being destroyed, even by the hands of their own brethren?

11. Yea, and if it had not been for his matchless power, and his mercy, and his long-suffering towards us, we should unavoidably have been cut off from the face of the earth long before this period of time, and perhaps been consigned to a state of endless misery and woe.

12. Behold, now I say unto you that he commandeth you to repent; and except ye repent, ye can in nowise inherit the kingdom of God. But behold, this is not all — he has commanded you to repent, or he will utterly destroy you from off the face of the earth; yea, he will visit you in his anger, and in his fierce anger he will not turn away.

13. Behold, do ye not remember the words which he spake unto Lehi, saying that: Inasmuch as ye shall keep my commandments, ye shall prosper in the land? And again it is said that: Inasmuch as ye will not keep my commandments ye shall be cut off from the presence of the Lord.

14. Now I would that ye should remember, that inasmuch as the Lamanites have not kept the commandments of God, they have been cut off from the presence of the Lord. Now we see that the word of the Lord has been verified in this thing, and the Lamanites have been cut off from his presence, from the beginning of their transgressions in the land.

15. Nevertheless I say unto you, that it shall be more tolerable for them in the day of judgment than for you, if ye remain in your sins, yea, and even more tolerable for them in this life than for you, except ye repent.

16. For there are many promises which are extended to the Lamanites; for it is because of the traditions of their fathers that caused them to remain in their state of ignorance; therefore the Lord will be merciful unto them and prolong their existence in the land.

17. And at some period of time they will be brought to believe in his word, and to know of the incorrectness of the traditions of their fathers; and many of them will be saved, for the Lord will be merciful unto all who call on his name.

18. But behold, I say unto you that if ye persist in your wickedness that your days shall not be prolonged in the land, for the Lamanites shall be sent upon you; and if ye repent not they shall come in a time when you know not, and ye shall be visited with utter destruction; and it shall be according to the fierce anger of the Lord.

19. For he will not suffer you that ye shall live in your iniquities, to destroy his people. I say unto you, Nay; he would rather suffer that the Lamanites might destroy all his people who are called the people of Nephi, if it were possible that they could fall into sins and transgressions, after having had so much light and so much knowledge given unto them of the Lord their God;

20. Yea, after having been such a highly favored people of the Lord; yea, after having been favored above every other nation, kindred, tongue, or people; after having had all things made known unto them, according to their desires, and their faith, and prayers, of that which has been, and which is, and which is to come;

21. Having been visited by the Spirit of God; having conversed with angels, and having been spoken unto by the voice of the Lord; and having the spirit of prophecy, and the spirit of revelation, and also many gifts, the gift of speaking with tongues, and the gift of preaching, and the gift of the Holy Ghost, and the gift of translation;

22. Yea, and after having been delivered of God out of the land of Jerusalem, by the hand of the Lord; having been saved from famine, and from sickness, and all manner of diseases of every kind; and they having waxed strong in battle, that they might not be destroyed; having been brought out of bondage time after time, and having been kept and preserved until now; and they have been prospered until they are rich in all manner of things —

23. And now behold I say unto you, that if this people, who have received so many blessings from the hand of the Lord, should transgress contrary to the light and knowledge which they do have, I say unto you that if this be the case, that if they should fall into transgression, it would be far more tolerable for the Lamanites than for them.

24. For behold, the promises of the Lord are extended to the Lamanites, but they are not unto you if ye transgress; for has not the Lord expressly promised and firmly decreed, that if ye will rebel against him that ye shall utterly be destroyed from off the face of the earth?

25. And now for this cause, that ye may not be destroyed, the Lord has sent his angel to visit many of his people, declaring unto them that they must go forth and cry mightily unto this people, saying: Repent ye, for the kingdom of heaven is nigh at hand;

26. And not many days hence the Son of God shall come in his glory; and his glory shall be the glory of the Only Begotten of the Father, full of grace, equity, and truth, full of patience, mercy, and long-suffering, quick to hear the cries of his people and to answer their prayers.

27. And behold, he cometh to redeem those who will be baptized unto repentance, through faith on his name.

28. Therefore, prepare ye the way of the Lord, for

the time is at hand that all men shall reap a reward of their works, according to that which they have been — if they have been righteous they shall reap the salvation of their souls, according to the power and deliverance of Jesus Christ; and if they have been evil they shall reap the damnation of their souls, according to the power and captivation of the devil.

29. Now behold, this is the voice of the angel, crying unto the people.

30. And now, my beloved brethren, for ye are my brethren, and ye ought to be beloved, and ye ought to bring forth works which are meet for repentance, seeing that your hearts have been grossly hardened against the word of God, and seeing that ye are a lost and a fallen people.

31. Now it came to pass that when I, Alma, had spoken these words, behold, the people were wroth with me because I said unto them that they were a hardhearted and a stiffnecked people.

32. And also because I said unto them that they were a lost and a fallen people they were angry with me, and sought to lay their hands upon me, that they might cast me into prison.

33. But it came to pass that the Lord did not suffer them that they should take me at that time and cast me into prison.

34. And it came to pass that Amulek went and stood forth, and began to preach unto them also. And now the words of Amulek are not all written, nevertheless a part of his words are written in this book.

CHAPTER 10.

1. Now these are the words which Amulek preached unto the people who were in the land of Ammonihah, saying:

2. I am Amulek; I am the son of Giddonah, who was the son of Ishmael, who was a descendant of Aminadi; and it was the same Aminadi who interpreted the writing which was upon the wall of the temple, which was written by the finger of God.

3. And Aminadi was a descendant of Nephi, who was the son of Lehi, who came out of the land of Jerusalem, who was a descendant of Manasseh, who was the son of Joseph who was sold into Egypt by the hands of his brethren.

4. And behold, I am also a man of no small reputation among all those who know me; yea, and behold, I have many kindreds and friends, and I have also acquired much riches by the hand of my industry.

5. Nevertheless, after all this, I never have known much of the ways of the Lord, and his mysteries and marvelous power. I said I never had known much of these things; but behold, I mistake, for I have seen much of his mysteries and his marvelous power; yea, even in the preservation of the lives of this people.

6. Nevertheless, I did harden my heart, for I was called many times and I would not hear; therefore I knew concerning these things, yet I would not know; therefore I went on rebelling against God, in the wickedness of my heart, even until the fourth day of this seventh month, which is in the tenth year of the reign of the judges.

7. As I was journeying to see a very near kindred, behold an angel of the Lord appeared unto me and said: Amulek, return to thine own house, for thou shalt feed a prophet of the Lord; yea, a holy man, who is a chosen man of God; for he has fasted many days because of the sins of this people, and he is an hungered, and thou shalt receive him into thy house and feed him, and he shall bless thee and thy house; and the blessing of the Lord shall rest upon thee and thy house.

8. And it came to pass that I obeyed the voice of the angel, and returned towards my house. And as I was going thither I found the man whom the angel said unto me: Thou shalt receive into thy house — and behold it was this same man who has been speaking unto you concerning the things of God.

9. And the angel said unto me he is a holy man; wherefore I know he is a holy man because it was said by an angel of God.

10. And again, I know that the things whereof he hath testified are true; for behold I say unto you, that as the Lord liveth, even so has he sent his angel to make these things manifest unto me; and this he has done while this Alma hath dwelt at my house.

11. For behold, he hath blessed mine house, he hath blessed me, and my women, and my children, and my father and my kinsfolk; yea, even all my kindred hath he blessed, and the blessing of the Lord hath rested upon us according to the words which he spake.

12. And now, when Amulek had spoken these words the people began to be astonished, seeing there was more than one witness who testified of the things whereof they were accused, and also of the things which were to come, according to the spirit of prophecy which was in them.

13. Nevertheless, there were some among them who thought to question them, that by their cunning devices they might catch them in their words, that they might find witness against them, that they might deliver them to their judges that they might be judged according to the law, and that they might be slain or cast into prison, according to the crime which they could make appear or witness against them.

14. Now it was those men who sought to destroy them, who were lawyers, who were hired or appointed by the people to administer the law at their times of trials,

or at the trials of the crimes of the people before the judges.

15. Now these lawyers were learned in all the arts and cunning of the people; and this was to enable them that they might be skilful in their profession.

16. And it came to pass that they began to question Amulek, that thereby they might make him cross his words, or contradict the words which he should speak.

17. Now they knew not that Amulek could know of their designs. But it came to pass as they began to question him, he perceived their thoughts, and he said unto them: O ye wicked and perverse generation, ye lawyers and hypocrites, for ye are laying the foundation of the devil; for ye are laying traps and snares to catch the holy ones of God.

18. Ye are laying plans to pervert the ways of the righteous, and to bring down the wrath of God upon your heads, even to the utter destruction of this people.

19. Yea, well did Mosiah say, who was our last king, when he was about to deliver up the kingdom, having no one to confer it upon, causing that this people should be governed by their own voices—yea, well did he say that if the time should come that the voice of this people should choose iniquity, that is, if the time should come that this people should fall into transgression, they would be ripe for destruction.

20. And now I say unto you that well doth the Lord judge of your iniquities; well doth he cry unto this people, by the voice of his angels: Repent ye, repent, for the kingdom of heaven is at hand.

21. Yea, well doth he cry, by the voice of his angels that: I will come down among my people, with equity and justice in my hands.

22. Yea, and I say unto you that if it were not for the prayers of the righteous, who are now in the land, that ye would even now be visited with utter destruction; yet it would not be by flood, as were the people in the days of Noah, but it would be by famine, and by pestilence, and the sword.

23. But it is by the prayers of the righteous that ye are spared; now therefore, if ye will cast out the righteous from among you then will not the Lord stay his hand; but in his fierce anger he will come out against you; then ye shall be smitten by famine, and by pestilence, and by the sword; and the time is soon at hand except ye repent.

24. And now it came to pass that the people were more angry with Amulek, and they cried out, saying: This man doth revile against our laws which are just, and our wise lawyers whom we have selected.

25. But Amulek stretched forth his hand, and cried the mightier unto them, saying: O ye wicked and perverse generation, why hath Satan got such great hold upon your hearts? Why will ye yield yourselves unto him that he may have power over you, to blind your eyes, that ye will not understand the words which are spoken, according to their truth?

26. For behold, have I testified against your law? Ye do not understand; ye say that I have spoken against your law; but I have not, but I have spoken in favor of your law, to your condemnation.

27. And now behold, I say unto you, that the foundation of the destruction of this people is beginning to be laid by the unrighteousness of your lawyers and your judges.

28. And now it came to pass that when Amulek had spoken these words the people cried out against him, saying: Now we know that this man is a child of the devil, for he hath lied unto us; for he hath spoken against our law. And now he says that he has not spoken against it.

29. And again, he has reviled against our lawyers, and our judges.

30. And it came to pass that the lawyers put it into their hearts that they should remember these things against him.

31. And there was one among them whose name was Zeezrom. Now he was the foremost to accuse Amulek and Alma, he being one of the most expert among them, having much business to do among the people.

32. Now the object of these lawyers was to get gain; and they got gain according to their employ.

CHAPTER 11.

1. Now it was in the law of Mosiah that every man who was a judge of the law, or those who were appointed to be judges, should receive wages according to the time which they labored to judge those who were brought before them to be judged.

2. Now if a man owed another, and he would not pay that which he did owe, he was complained of to the judge; and the judge executed authority, and sent forth officers that the man should be brought before him; and he judged the man according to the law and the evidences which were brought against him, and thus the man was compelled to pay that which he owed, or be stripped, or be cast out from among the people as a thief and a robber.

3. And the judge received for his wages according to his time—a senine of gold for a day, or a senum of silver, which is equal to a senine of gold; and this is according to the law which was given.

4. Now these are the names of the different pieces of their gold, and of their silver, according to their value. And the names are given by the Nephites, for they did not reckon after the manner of the Jews who were at Jerusalem; neither did they measure after the manner of the Jews; but they altered their reckoning and their measure, ac-

cording to the minds and the circumstances of the people, in every generation, until the reign of the judges, they having been established by king Mosiah.

5. Now the reckoning is thus—a senine of gold, a seon of gold, a shum of gold, and a limnah of gold.

6. A senum of silver, an amnor of silver, an ezrom of silver, and an onti of silver.

7. A senum of silver was equal to a senine of gold, and either for a measure of barley, and also for a measure of every kind of grain.

8. Now the amount of a seon of gold was twice the value of a senine.

9. And a shum of gold was twice the value of a seon.

10. And a limnah of gold was the value of them all.

11. And an amnor of silver was as great as two senums.

12. And an ezrom of silver was as great as four senums.

13. And an onti was as great as them all.

14. Now this is the value of the lesser numbers of their reckoning—

15. A shiblon is half of a senum; therefore, a shiblon for half a measure of barley.

16. And a shiblum is a half of a shiblon.

17. And a leah is the half of a shiblum.

18. Now this is their number, according to their reckoning.

19. Now an antion of gold is equal to three shiblons.

20. Now, it was for the sole purpose to get gain, because they received their wages according to their employ, therefore, they did stir up the people to riotings, and all manner of disturbances and wickedness, that they might have more employ, that they might get money according to the suits which were brought before them; therefore they did stir up the people against Alma and Amulek.

21. And this Zeezrom began to question Amulek, saying: Will ye answer me a few questions which I shall ask you? Now Zeezrom was a man who was expert in the devices of the devil, that he might destroy that which was good; therefore, he said unto Amulek: Will ye answer the questions which I shall put unto you?

22. And Amulek said unto him: Yea, if it be according to the Spirit of the Lord, which is in me; for I shall say nothing which is contrary to the Spirit of the Lord. And Zeezrom said unto him: Behold, here are six onties of silver, and all these will I give thee if thou wilt deny the existence of a Supreme Being.

23. Now Amulek said: O thou child of hell, why tempt ye me? Knowest thou that the righteous yieldeth to no such temptations?

24. Believest thou that there is no God? I say unto you, Nay, thou knowest that there is a God, but thou lovest that lucre more than him.

25. And now thou hast lied before God unto me. Thou saidst unto me—Behold these six onties, which are of great worth, I will give unto thee—when thou hadst it in thy heart to retain them from me; and it was only thy desire that I should deny the true and living God, that thou mightest have cause to destroy me. And now behold, for this great evil thou shalt have thy reward.

26. And Zeezrom said unto him: Thou sayest there is a true and living God?

27. And Amulek said: Yea, there is a true and living God.

28. Now Zeezrom said: Is there more than one God?

29. And he answered, No.

30. Now Zeezrom said unto him again: How knowest thou these things?

31. And he said: An angel hath made them known unto me.

32. And Zeezrom said again: Who is he that shall come? Is it the Son of God?

33. And he said unto him, Yea.

34. And Zeezrom said again: Shall he save his people in their sins? And Amulek answered and said unto him: I say unto you he shall not, for it is impossible for him to deny his word.

35. Now Zeezrom said unto the people: See that ye remember these things; for he said there is but one God; yet he saith that the Son of God shall come, but he shall not save his people—as though he had authority to command God.

36. Now Amulek saith again unto him: Behold thou hast lied, for thou sayest that I spake as though I had authority to command God because I said he shall not save his people in their sins.

37. And I say unto you again that he cannot save them in their sins; for I cannot deny his word, and he hath said that no unclean thing can inherit the kingdom of heaven; therefore, how can ye be saved, except ye inherit the kingdom of heaven? Therefore, ye cannot be saved in your sins.

38. Now Zeezrom saith again unto him: Is the Son of God the very Eternal Father?

39. And Amulek said unto him: Yea, he is the very Eternal Father of heaven and of earth, and all things which in them are; he is the beginning and the end, the first and the last;

40. And he shall come into the world to redeem his people; and he shall take upon him the transgressions of those who believe on his name; and these are they that shall have eternal life, and salvation cometh to none else.

41. Therefore the wicked remain as though there had been no redemption made, except it be the loosing of

the bands of death; for behold, the day cometh that all shall rise from the dead and stand before God, and be judged according to their works.

42. Now, there is a death which is called a temporal death; and the death of Christ shall loose the bands of this temporal death, that all shall be raised from this temporal death.

43. The spirit and the body shall be reunited again in its perfect form; both limb and joint shall be restored to its proper frame, even as we now are at this time; and we shall be brought to stand before God, knowing even as we know now, and have a bright recollection of all our guilt.

44. Now, this restoration shall come to all, both old and young, both bond and free, both male and female, both the wicked and the righteous; and even there shall not so much as a hair of their heads be lost; but every thing shall be restored to its perfect frame, as it is now, or in the body, and shall be brought and be arraigned before the bar of Christ the Son, and God the Father, and the Holy Spirit, which is one Eternal God, to be judged according to their works, whether they be good or whether they be evil.

45. Now, behold, I have spoken unto you concerning the death of the mortal body, and also concerning the resurrection of the mortal body. I say unto you that this mortal body is raised to an immortal body, that is from death, even from the first death unto life, that they can die no more; their spirits uniting with their bodies, never to be divided; thus the whole becoming spiritual and immortal, that they can no more see corruption.

46. Now, when Amulek had finished these words the people began again to be astonished, and also Zeezrom began to tremble. And thus ended the words of Amulek, or this is all that I have written.

CHAPTER 12.

1. Now Alma, seeing that the words of Amulek had silenced Zeezrom, for he beheld that Amulek had caught him in his lying and deceiving to destroy him, and seeing that he began to tremble under a consciousness of his guilt, he opened his mouth and began to speak unto him, and to establish the words of Amulek, and to explain things beyond, or to unfold the scriptures beyond that which Amulek had done.

2. Now the words that Alma spake unto Zeezrom were heard by the people round about; for the multitude was great, and he spake on this wise:

3. Now Zeezrom, seeing that thou hast been taken in thy lying and craftiness, for thou hast not lied unto men only but thou hast lied unto God; for behold, he knows all thy thoughts, and thou seest that thy thoughts are made known unto us by his Spirit;

4. And thou seest that we know that thy plan was a very subtle plan, as to the subtlety of the devil, for to lie and to deceive this people that thou mightest set them against us, to revile us and to cast us out—

5. Now this was a plan of thine adversary, and he hath exercised his power in thee. Now I would that ye should remember that what I say unto thee I say unto all.

6. And behold I say unto you all that this was a snare of the adversary, which he has laid to catch this people, that he might bring you into subjection unto him, that he might encircle you about with his chains, that he might chain you down to everlasting destruction, according to the power of his captivity.

7. Now when Alma had spoken these words, Zeezrom began to tremble more exceedingly, for he was convinced more and more of the power of God; and he was also convinced that Alma and Amulek had a knowledge of him, for he was convinced that they knew the thoughts and intents of his heart; for power was given unto them that they might know of these things according to the spirit of prophecy.

8. And Zeezrom began to inquire of them diligently, that he might know more concerning the kingdom of God. And he said unto Alma: What does this mean which Amulek hath spoken concerning the resurrection of the dead, that all shall rise from the dead, both the just and the unjust, and are brought to stand before God to be judged according to their works?

9. And now Alma began to expound these things unto him, saying: It is given unto many to know the mysteries of God; nevertheless they are laid under a strict command that they shall not impart only according to the portion of his word which he doth grant unto the children of men, according to the heed and diligence which they give unto him.

10. And therefore, he that will harden his heart, the same receiveth the lesser portion of the word; and he that will not harden his heart, to him is given the greater portion of the word, until it is given unto him to know the mysteries of God until he know them in full.

11. And they that will harden their hearts, to them is given the lesser portion of the word until they know nothing concerning his mysteries; and then they are taken captive by the devil, and led by his will down to destruction. Now this is what is meant by the chains of hell.

12. And Amulek hath spoken plainly concerning death, and being raised from this mortality to a state of immortality, and being brought before the bar of God, to be judged according to our works.

13. Then if our hearts have been hardened, yea, if we have hardened our hearts against the word, insomuch that it has not been found in us, then will our state be

awful, for then we shall be condemned.

14. For our words will condemn us, yea, all our works will condemn us; we shall not be found spotless; and our thoughts will also condemn us; and in this awful state we shall not dare to look up to our God; and we would fain be glad if we could command the rocks and the mountains to fall upon us to hide us from his presence.

15. But this cannot be; we must come forth and stand before him in his glory, and in his power, and in his might, majesty, and dominion, and acknowledge to our everlasting shame that all his judgments are just; that he is just in all his works, and that he is merciful unto the children of men, and that he has all power to save every man that believeth on his name and bringeth forth fruit meet for repentance.

16. And now behold, I say unto you then cometh a death, even a second death, which is a spiritual death; then is a time that whosoever dieth in his sins, as to a temporal death, shall also die a spiritual death; yea, he shall die as to things pertaining unto righteousness.

17. Then is the time when their torments shall be as a lake of fire and brimstone, whose flame ascendeth up forever and ever; and then is the time that they shall be chained down to an everlasting destruction, according to the power and captivity of Satan, he having subjected them according to his will.

18. Then, I say unto you, they shall be as though there had been no redemption made; for they cannot be redeemed according to God's justice; and they cannot die, seeing there is no more corruption.

19. Now it came to pass that when Alma had made an end of speaking these words, the people began to be more astonished;

20. But there was one Antionah, who was a chief ruler among them, came forth and said unto him: What is this that thou hast said, that man should rise from the dead and be changed from this mortal to an immortal state that the soul can never die?

21. What does the scripture mean, which saith that God placed cherubim and a flaming sword on the east of the garden of Eden, lest our first parents should enter and partake of the fruit of the tree of life, and live forever? And thus we see that there was no possible chance that they should live forever.

22. Now Alma said unto him: This is the thing which I was about to explain. Now we see that Adam did fall by the partaking of the forbidden fruit, according to the word of God; and thus we see, that by his fall, all mankind became a lost and fallen people.

23. And now behold, I say unto you that if it had been possible for Adam to have partaken of the fruit of the tree of life at that time, there would have been no death,

and the word would have been void, making God a liar, for he said: If thou eat thou shalt surely die.

24. And we see that death comes upon mankind, yea, the death which has been spoken of by Amulek, which is the temporal death; nevertheless there was a space granted unto man in which he might repent; therefore this life became a probationary state; a time to prepare to meet God; a time to prepare for that endless state which has been spoken of by us, which is after the resurrection of the dead.

25. Now, if it had not been for the plan of redemption, which was laid from the foundation of the world, there could have been no resurrection of the dead; but there was a plan of redemption laid, which shall bring to pass the resurrection of the dead, of which has been spoken.

26. And now behold, if it were possible that our first parents could have gone forth and partaken of the tree of life they would have been forever miserable, having no preparatory state; and thus the plan of redemption would have been frustrated, and the word of God would have been void, taking none effect.

27. But behold, it was not so; but it was appointed unto men that they must die; and after death, they must come to judgment, even that same judgment of which we have spoken, which is the end.

28. And after God had appointed that these things should come unto man, behold, then he saw that it was expedient that man should know concerning the things whereof he had appointed unto them;

29. Therefore he sent angels to converse with them, who caused men to behold of his glory.

30. And they began from that time forth to call on his name; therefore God conversed with men, and made known unto them the plan of redemption, which had been prepared from the foundation of the world; and this he made known unto them according to their faith and repentance and their holy works.

31. Wherefore, he gave commandments unto men, they having first transgressed the first commandments as to things which were temporal, and becoming as Gods, knowing good from evil, placing themselves in a state to act, or being placed in a state to act according to their wills and pleasures, whether to do evil or to do good—

32. Therefore God gave unto them commandments, after having made known unto them the plan of redemption, that they should not do evil, the penalty thereof being a second death, which was an everlasting death as to things pertaining unto righteousness; for on such the plan of redemption could have no power, for the works of justice could not be destroyed, according to the supreme goodness of God.

33. But God did call on men, in the name of his

Son, (this being the plan of redemption which was laid) saying: If ye will repent, and harden not your hearts, then will I have mercy upon you, through mine Only Begotten Son;

34. Therefore, whosoever repenteth, and hardeneth not his heart, he shall have claim on mercy through mine Only Begotten Son, unto a remission of his sins; and these shall enter into my rest.

35. And whosoever will harden his heart and will do iniquity, behold, I swear in my wrath that he shall not enter into my rest.

36. And now, my brethren, behold I say unto you, that if ye will harden your hearts ye shall not enter into the rest of the Lord; therefore your iniquity provoketh him that he sendeth down his wrath upon you as in the first provocation, yea, according to his word in the last provocation as well as the first, to the everlasting destruction of your souls; therefore, according to his word, unto the last death, as well as the first.

37. And now, my brethren, seeing we know these things, and they are true, let us repent, and harden not our hearts, that we provoke not the Lord our God to pull down his wrath upon us in these his second commandments which he has given unto us; but let us enter into the rest of God, which is prepared according to his word.

CHAPTER 13.

1. And again, my brethren, I would cite your minds forward to the time when the Lord God gave these commandments unto his children; and I would that ye should remember that the Lord God ordained priests, after his holy order, which was after the order of his Son, to teach these things unto the people.

2. And those priests were ordained after the order of his Son, in a manner that thereby the people might know in what manner to look forward to his Son for redemption.

3. And this is the manner after which they were ordained—being called and prepared from the foundation of the world according to the foreknowledge of God, on account of their exceeding faith and good works; in the first place being left to choose good or evil; therefore they having chosen good, and exercising exceeding great faith, are called with a holy calling, yea, with that holy calling which was prepared with, and according to, a preparatory redemption for such.

4. And thus they have been called to this holy calling on account of their faith, while others would reject the Spirit of God on account of the hardness of their hearts and blindness of their minds, while, if it had not been for this they might have had as great privilege as their brethren.

5. Or in fine, in the first place they were on the same standing with their brethren; thus this holy calling being prepared from the foundation of the world for such as would not harden their hearts, being in and through the atonement of the Only Begotten Son, who was prepared—

6. And thus being called by this holy calling, and ordained unto the high priesthood of the holy order of God, to teach his commandments unto the children of men, that they also might enter into his rest—

7. This high priesthood being after the order of his Son, which order was from the foundation of the world; or in other words, being without beginning of days or end of years, being prepared from eternity to all eternity, according to his foreknowledge of all things—

8. Now they were ordained after this manner—being called with a holy calling, and ordained with a holy ordinance, and taking upon them the high priesthood of the holy order, which calling, and ordinance, and high priesthood, is without beginning or end—

9. Thus they become high priests forever, after the order of the Son, the Only Begotten of the Father, who is without beginning of days or end of years, who is full of grace, equity, and truth. And thus it is. Amen.

10. Now, as I said concerning the holy order of this high priesthood, there were many who were ordained and became high priests of God; and it was on account of their exceeding faith and repentance, and their righteousness before God, they choosing to repent and work righteousness rather than to perish;

11. Therefore they were called after this holy order, and were sanctified, and their garments were washed white through the blood of the Lamb.

12. Now they, after being sanctified by the Holy Ghost, having their garments made white, being pure and spotless before God, could not look upon sin save it were with abhorrence; and there were many, exceeding great many, who were made pure and entered into the rest of the Lord their God.

13. And now, my brethren, I would that ye should humble yourselves before God, and bring forth fruit meet for repentance, that ye may also enter into that rest.

14. Yea, humble yourselves even as the people in the days of Melchizedek, who was also a high priest after this same order which I have spoken, who also took upon him the high priesthood forever.

15. And it was this same Melchizedek to whom Abraham paid tithes; yea, even our father Abraham paid tithes of one-tenth part of all he possessed.

16. Now these ordinances were given after this manner, that thereby the people might look forward on the Son of God, it being a type of his order, or it being his order, and this that they might look forward to him for a

remission of their sins, that they might enter into the rest of the Lord.

17. Now this Melchizedek was a king over the land of Salem; and his people had waxed strong in iniquity and abomination; yea, they had all gone astray; they were full of all manner of wickedness;

18. But Melchizedek having exercised mighty faith, and received the office of the high priesthood according to the holy order of God, did preach repentance unto his people. And behold, they did repent; and Melchizedek did establish peace in the land in his days; therefore he was called the prince of peace, for he was the king of Salem; and he did reign under his father.

19. Now, there were many before him, and also there were many afterwards, but none were greater; therefore, of him they have more particularly made mention.

20. Now I need not rehearse the matter; what I have said may suffice. Behold, the scriptures are before you; if ye will wrest them it shall be to your own destruction.

21. And now it came to pass that when Alma had said these words unto them, he stretched forth his hand unto them and cried with a mighty voice, saying: Now is the time to repent, for the day of salvation draweth nigh;

22. Yea, and the voice of the Lord, by the mouth of angels, doth declare it unto all nations; yea, doth declare it, that they may have glad tidings of great joy; yea, and he doth sound these glad tidings among all his people, yea, even to them that are scattered abroad upon the face of the earth; wherefore they have come unto us.

23. And they are made known unto us in plain terms, that we may understand, that we cannot err; and this because of our being wanderers in a strange land; therefore, we are thus highly favored, for we have these glad tidings declared unto us in all parts of our vineyard.

24. For behold, angels are declaring it unto many at this time in our land; and this is for the purpose of preparing the hearts of the children of men to receive his word at the time of his coming in his glory.

25. And now we only wait to hear the joyful news declared unto us by the mouth of angels, of his coming; for the time cometh, we know not how soon. Would to God that it might be in my day; but let it be sooner or later, in it I will rejoice.

26. And it shall be made known unto just and holy men, by the mouth of angels, at the time of his coming, that the words of our fathers may be fulfilled, according to that which they have spoken concerning him, which was according to the spirit of prophecy which was in them.

27. And now, my brethren, I wish from the inmost part of my heart, yea, with great anxiety even unto pain, that ye would hearken unto my words, and cast off your sins, and not procrastinate the day of your repentance;

28. But that ye would humble yourselves before the

Lord, and call on his holy name, and watch and pray continually, that ye may not be tempted above that which ye can bear, and thus be led by the Holy Spirit, becoming humble, meek, submissive, patient, full of love and all long-suffering;

29. Having faith on the Lord; having a hope that ye shall receive eternal life; having the love of God always in your hearts, that ye may be lifted up at the last day and enter into his rest.

30. And may the Lord grant unto you repentance, that ye may not bring down his wrath upon you, that ye may not be bound down by the chains of hell, that ye may not suffer the second death.

31. And Alma spake many more words unto the people, which are not written in this book.

CHAPTER 14.

1. And it came to pass after he had made an end of speaking unto the people many of them did believe on his words, and began to repent, and to search the scriptures.

2. But the more part of them were desirous that they might destroy Alma and Amulek; for they were angry with Alma, because of the plainness of his words unto Zeezrom; and they also said that Amulek had lied unto them, and had reviled against their law and also against their lawyers and judges.

3. And they were also angry with Alma and Amulek; and because they had testified so plainly against their wickedness, they sought to put them away privily.

4. But it came to pass that they did not; but they took them and bound them with strong cords, and took them before the chief judge of the land.

5. And the people went forth and witnessed against them—testifying that they had reviled against the law, and their lawyers and judges of the land, and also of all the people that were in the land; and also testified that there was but one God, and that he should send his Son among the people, but he should not save them; and many such things did the people testify against Alma and Amulek. Now this was done before the chief judge of the land.

6. And it came to pass that Zeezrom was astonished at the words which had been spoken; and he also knew concerning the blindness of the minds, which he had caused among the people by his lying words; and his soul began to be harrowed up under a consciousness of his own guilt; yea, he began to be encircled about by the pains of hell.

7. And it came to pass that he began to cry unto the people, saying: Behold, I am guilty, and these men are spotless before God. And he began to plead for them from that time forth; but they reviled him, saying: Art thou also possessed with the devil? And they spit upon him, and cast him out from among them, and also all those who be-

lieved in the words which had been spoken by Alma and Amulek; and they cast them out, and sent men to cast stones at them.

8. And they brought their wives and children together, and whosoever believed or had been taught to believe in the word of God they caused that they should be cast into the fire, and they also brought forth their records which contained the holy scriptures, and cast them into the fire also, that they might be burned and destroyed by fire.

9. And it came to pass that they took Alma and Amulek, and carried them forth to the place of martyrdom, that they might witness the destruction of those who were consumed by fire.

10. And when Amulek saw the pains of the women and children who were consuming in the fire, he also was pained; and he said unto Alma: How can we witness this awful scene? Therefore let us stretch forth our hands, and exercise the power of God which is in us, and save them from the flames.

11. But Alma said unto him: The Spirit constraineth me that I must not stretch forth mine hand; for behold the Lord receiveth them up unto himself, in glory; and he doth suffer that they may do this thing, or that the people may do this thing unto them, according to the hardness of their hearts, that the judgments which he shall exercise upon them in his wrath may be just; and the blood of the innocent shall stand as a witness against them, yea, and cry mightily against them at the last day.

12. Now Amulek said unto Alma: Behold, perhaps they will burn us also.

13. And Alma said: Be it according to the will of the Lord. But, behold, our work is not finished; therefore they burn us not.

14. Now it came to pass that when the bodies of those who had been cast into the fire were consumed, and also the records which were cast in with them, the chief judge of the land came and stood before Alma and Amulek, as they were bound; and he smote them with his hand upon their cheeks, and said unto them: After what ye have seen, will ye preach again unto this people, that they shall be cast into a lake of fire and brimstone?

15. Behold, ye see that ye had not power to save those who had been cast into the fire; neither has God saved them because they were of thy faith. And the judge smote them again upon their cheeks, and asked: What say ye for yourselves?

16. Now this judge was after the order and faith of Nehor, who slew Gideon.

17. And it came to pass that Alma and Amulek answered him nothing; and he smote them again, and delivered them to the officers to be cast into prison.

18. And when they had been cast into prison three days, there came many lawyers, and judges, and priests, and teachers, who were of the profession of Nehor; and they came in unto the prison to see them, and they questioned them about many words; but they answered them nothing.

19. And it came to pass that the judge stood before them, and said: Why do ye not answer the words of this people? Know ye not that I have power to deliver you up unto the flames? And he commanded them to speak; but they answered nothing.

20. And it came to pass that they departed and went their ways, but came again on the morrow; and the judge also smote them again on their cheeks. And many came forth also, and smote them, saying: Will ye stand again and judge this people, and condemn our law? If ye have such great power why do ye not deliver yourselves?

21. And many such things did they say unto them, gnashing their teeth upon them, and spitting upon them, and saying: How shall we look when we are damned?

22. And many such things, yea, all manner of such things did they say unto them; and thus they did mock them for many days. And they did withhold food from them that they might hunger, and water that they might thirst; and they also did take from them their clothes that they were naked; and thus they were bound with strong cords, and confined in prison.

23. And it came to pass after they had thus suffered for many days, (and it was on the twelfth day, in the tenth month, in the tenth year of the reign of the judges over the people of Nephi) that the chief judge over the land of Ammonihah and many of their teachers and their lawyers went in unto the prison where Alma and Amulek were bound with cords.

24. And the chief judge stood before them, and smote them again, and said unto them: If ye have the power of God deliver yourselves from these bands, and then we will believe that the Lord will destroy this people according to your words.

25. And it came to pass that they all went forth and smote them, saying the same words, even until the last; and when the last had spoken unto them the power of God was upon Alma and Amulek, and they rose and stood upon their feet.

26. And Alma cried, saying: How long shall we suffer these great afflictions, O Lord? O Lord, give us strength according to our faith which is in Christ, even unto deliverance. And they broke the cords with which they were bound; and when the people saw this, they began to flee, for the fear of destruction had come upon them.

27. And it came to pass that so great was their fear that they fell to the earth, and did not obtain the outer door of the prison; and the earth shook mightily, and the walls of the prison were rent in twain, so that they fell

to the earth; and the chief judge, and the lawyers, and priests, and teachers, who smote upon Alma and Amulek, were slain by the fall thereof.

28. And Alma and Amulek came forth out of the prison, and they were not hurt; for the Lord had granted unto them power, according to their faith which was in Christ. And they straightway came forth out of the prison; and they were loosed from their bands; and the prison had fallen to the earth, and every soul within the walls thereof, save it were Alma and Amulek, was slain; and they straightway came forth into the city.

29. Now the people having heard a great noise came running together by multitudes to know the cause of it; and when they saw Alma and Amulek coming forth out of the prison, and the walls thereof had fallen to the earth, they were struck with great fear, and fled from the presence of Alma and Amulek even as a goat fleeth with her young from two lions; and thus they did flee from the presence of Alma and Amulek.

CHAPTER 15.

1. And it came to pass that Alma and Amulek were commanded to depart out of that city; and they departed, and came out even into the land of Sidom; and behold, there they found all the people who had departed out of the land of Ammonihah, who had been cast out and stoned, because they believed in the words of Alma.

2. And they related unto them all that had happened unto their wives and children, and also concerning themselves, and of their power of deliverance.

3. And also Zeezrom lay sick at Sidom, with a burning fever, which was caused by the great tribulations of his mind on account of his wickedness, for he supposed that Alma and Amulek were no more; and he supposed that they had been slain because of his iniquity. And this great sin, and his many other sins, did harrow up his mind until it did become exceeding sore, having no deliverance; therefore he began to be scorched with a burning heat.

4. Now, when he heard that Alma and Amulek were in the land of Sidom, his heart began to take courage; and he sent a message immediately unto them, desiring them to come unto him.

5. And it came to pass that they went immediately, obeying the message which he had sent unto them; and they went in unto the house unto Zeezrom; and they found him upon his bed, sick, being very low with a burning fever; and his mind also was exceeding sore because of his iniquities; and when he saw them he stretched forth his hand, and besought them that they would heal him.

6. And it came to pass that Alma said unto him, taking him by the hand: Believest thou in the power of Christ unto salvation?

7. And he answered and said: Yea, I believe all the words that thou hast taught.

8. And Alma said: If thou believest in the redemption of Christ thou canst be healed.

9. And he said: Yea, I believe according to thy words.

10. And then Alma cried unto the Lord, saying: O Lord our God, have mercy on this man, and heal him according to his faith which is in Christ.

11. And when Alma had said these words, Zeezrom leaped upon his feet, and began to walk; and this was done to the great astonishment of all the people; and the knowledge of this went forth throughout all the land of Sidom.

12. And Alma baptized Zeezrom unto the Lord; and he began from that time forth to preach unto the people.

13. And Alma established a church in the land of Sidom, and consecrated priests and teachers in the land, to baptize unto the Lord whosoever were desirous to be baptized.

14. And it came to pass that they were many; for they did flock in from all the region round about Sidom, and were baptized.

15. But as to the people that were in the land of Ammonihah, they yet remained a hard-hearted and a stiffnecked people; and they repented not of their sins, ascribing all the power of Alma and Amulek to the devil; for they were of the profession of Nehor, and did not believe in the repentance of their sins.

16. And it came to pass that Alma and Amulek, Amulek having forsaken all his gold, and silver, and his precious things, which were in the land of Ammonihah, for the word of God, he being rejected by those who were once his friends and also by his father and his kindred;

17. Therefore, after Alma having established the church at Sidom, seeing a great check, yea, seeing that the people were checked as to the pride of their hearts, and began to humble themselves before God, and began to assemble themselves together at their sanctuaries to worship God before the altar, watching and praying continually, that they might be delivered from Satan, and from death, and from destruction—

18. Now as I said, Alma having seen all these things, therefore he took Amulek and came over to the land of Zarahemla, and took him to his own house, and did administer unto him in his tribulations, and strengthened him in the Lord.

19. And thus ended the tenth year of the reign of the judges over the people of Nephi.

CHAPTER 16.

1. And it came to pass in the eleventh year of the reign of the judges over the people of Nephi, on the fifth

day of the second month, there having been much peace in the land of Zarahemla, there having been no wars nor contentions for a certain number of years, even until the fifth day of the second month in the eleventh year, there was a cry of war heard throughout the land.

2. For behold, the armies of the Lamanites had come in upon the wilderness side, into the borders of the land, even into the city of Ammonihah, and began to slay the people and destroy the city.

3. And now it came to pass, before the Nephites could raise a sufficient army to drive them out of the land, they had destroyed the people who were in the city of Ammonihah, and also some around the borders of Noah, and taken others captive into the wilderness.

4. Now it came to pass that the Nephites were desirous to obtain those who had been carried away captive into the wilderness.

5. Therefore, he that had been appointed chief captain over the armies of the Nephites, (and his name was Zoram, and he had two sons, Lehi and Aha)—now Zoram and his two sons, knowing that Alma was high priest over the church, and having heard that he had the spirit of prophecy, therefore they went unto him and desired of him to know whether the Lord would that they should go into the wilderness in search of their brethren, who had been taken captive by the Lamanites.

6. And it came to pass that Alma inquired of the Lord concerning the matter. And Alma returned and said unto them: Behold, the Lamanites will cross the river Sidon in the south wilderness, away up beyond the borders of the land of Manti. And behold there shall ye meet them, on the east of the river Sidon, and there the Lord will deliver unto thee thy brethren who have been taken captive by the Lamanites.

7. And it came to pass that Zoram and his sons crossed over the river Sidon, with their armies, and marched away beyond the borders of Manti into the south wilderness, which was on the east side of the river Sidon.

8. And they came upon the armies of the Lamanites, and the Lamanites were scattered and driven into the wilderness; and they took their brethren who had been taken captive by the Lamanites, and there was not one soul of them had been lost that were taken captive. And they were brought by their brethren to possess their own lands.

9. And thus ended the eleventh year of the judges, the Lamanites having been driven out of the land, and the people of Ammonihah were destroyed; yea, every living soul of the Ammonihahites was destroyed, and also their great city, which they said God could not destroy, because of its greatness.

10. But behold, in one day it was left desolate; and the carcasses were mangled by dogs and wild beasts of the wilderness.

11. Nevertheless, after many days their dead bodies were heaped up upon the face of the earth, and they were covered with a shallow covering. And now so great was the scent thereof that the people did not go in to possess the land of Ammonihah for many years. And it was called Desolation of Nehors; for they were of the profession of Nehor, who were slain; and their lands remained desolate.

12. And the Lamanites did not come again to war against the Nephites until the fourteenth year of the reign of the judges over the people of Nephi. And thus for three years did the people of Nephi have continual peace in all the land.

13. And Alma and Amulek went forth preaching repentance to the people in their temples, and in their sanctuaries, and also in their synagogues, which were built after the manner of the Jews.

14. And as many as would hear their words, unto them they did impart the word of God, without any respect of persons, continually.

15. And thus did Alma and Amulek go forth, and also many more who had been chosen for the work, to preach the word throughout all the land. And the establishment of the church became general throughout the land, in all the region round about, among all the people of the Nephites.

16. And there was no inequality among them; the Lord did pour out his Spirit on all the face of the land to prepare the minds of the children of men, or to prepare their hearts to receive the word which should be taught among them at the time of his coming—

17. That they might not be hardened against the word, that they might not be unbelieving, and go on to destruction, but that they might receive the word with joy, and as a branch be grafted into the true vine, that they might enter into the rest of the Lord their God.

18. Now those priests who did go forth among the people did preach against all lyings, and deceivings, and envyings, and strifes, and malice, and revilings, and stealing, robbing, plundering, murdering, committing adultery, and all manner of lasciviousness, crying that these things ought not so to be—

19. Holding forth things which must shortly come; yea, holding forth the coming of the Son of God, his sufferings and death, and also the resurrection of the dead.

20. And many of the people did inquire concerning the place where the Son of God should come; and they were taught that he would appear unto them after his resurrection; and this the people did hear with great joy and gladness.

21. And now after the church had been established throughout all the land—having got the victory over the devil, and the word of God being preached in its purity in all the land, and the Lord pouring out his blessings upon the people—thus ended the fourteenth year of the reign of the judges over the people of Nephi.

"Moroni's Challenge"

And when ye shall receive these things, I would exhort you that ye would ask God, the Eternal Father, in the name of Christ, if these things are not true; and if ye shall ask with a sincere heart, with real intent, having faith in Christ, he will manifest the truth of it unto you, by the power of the Holy Ghost. Moroni 10:4.

PREVIEW OF VOLUME IX

You will not want to miss the drama of Alma's missionary companions, Ammon, Aaron and others as they recount their thrilling experiences in Volume 9 of *Illustrated Stories from the Book of Mormon.*